PRINCIPLES, POLITICS, AND FUNDAMENTAL LAW

Selected Essays

Principles, Politics, and Fundamental Law

Selected Essays

HERBERT WECHSLER
Harlan Fiske Stone Professor of Constitutional Law
Columbia Law School

1961

HARVARD UNIVERSITY PRESS
Cambridge, Massachusetts

Distributed in Great Britain
by Oxford University Press, London

Library of Congress Catalog Card Number 61-5581

PRINTED IN THE UNITED STATES OF AMERICA

To

SAMUEL WECHSLER

of the New York Bar

with more than filial affection

PREFACE

I am grateful to my friends and former colleagues of the Harvard Law School Faculty for their nomination as Holmes lecturer for 1958–59. Their invitation was a needed stimulant to writing what for years I had been teaching but had never formally expressed.

My wife and I treasure a glowing recollection of the warm reception given us on the occasion of the lecture and our happy luncheon on that day with the Justices of the Supreme Judicial Court of Massachusetts. For this, too, I express my thanks.

I am indebted for permission to reprint or quote published material to the *Columbia Law Review*, the *Harvard Law Review*, the *Political Science Quarterly*, *Fortune Magazine*, the *American Bar Association Journal*, and Doubleday & Co., Inc.

Herbert Wechsler

Columbia Law School
March 28, 1960

CONTENTS

INTRODUCTION

The interest of the Press in publishing my Oliver Wendell Holmes lecture has given me the opportunity to resurrect three other papers on related themes from the recondite journals where they now repose. All of the essays are concerned with our national effort to govern our polity by fundamental law — an effort that demands self-consciousness about the nature of such law and its relation to politics. Written, as the papers were, at different times for different purposes, they make no claim to systematic treatment of the subject. In dealing with abiding problems of this kind, there may, however, be some virtue in a presentation that purports to be suggestive only. That is, in any case, the hope that animates the publication of this volume.

Two of the papers are addressed to the role of the Supreme Court in the interpretation of the Constitution and to the Court's discharge of that august responsibility. "Toward Neutral Principles of Constitutional Law" attempts to formulate, and in some measure to apply to current controversies, the minimal criteria of a defensible interpretative judgment. "Stone and the Constitution" recalls the crisis of the 1930's and its judicial settlement as it appeared in 1946, viewed through the work of one of the chief protagonists of the positions that prevailed. Others may find, as I do, that in thinking of the issues of today those of a quarter of a century ago are usefully remembered; there are both differences and similarities that should be weighed.

The importance of the Court as arbiter of constitutional disputes has led us sometimes to forget that it is not alone through its adjudications that the Constitution influences our society. In "The Political Safeguards of Federalism," I point to phases of our constitutionalism in which the Court is not involved but which provide the structural determinants of government and politics. Such constitutional provisions as those governing the composition and election of the Congress and the way in which we choose a President have a significance transcending that of anything the Court decides. They present problems no less challenging than those that may arise in litigation.

Though it places in jeopardy the unity of these related topics, I have included a fourth paper dealing with the very different subject of the war crimes trial at Nuremberg. My purpose is not only to reiterate a defense of the trial and judgment that the passing years have not induced me to repent, despite the vogue that hindsight has accorded their disparagement. The more important point is that the prosecution yields a testing case of what the striving for legality entails. In "The Issues of the Nuremberg Trial," I undertake to show how far, in the remote and unreal setting of the International Military Tribunal, neutrality and generality of principle emerged as the instrinsic qualities of law and prime constituents of a judicial action. The case has an important bearing, therefore, on the central thesis of "Toward Neutral Principles." It has a bearing also on the larger question of when law and legal method are appropriate and useful means for building foreign policy. Given the principles that we affirmed and acted on at Nuremberg as *legal* principles, could our response to Korea, on the one hand, or to Suez on the other, really have been different than it was?

In reconsidering these papers for the present publication, I have made small corrections and additions of detail. Neither my further thoughts nor any subsequent developments have been sufficiently extensive to require general revision. There are, however, a few matters that I have reserved for mention here.

(1) Some of those who heard or read "Toward Neutral Principles" have doubted whether "neutral" is the proper word to designate the quality I have in mind or whether its intended meaning is made clear. I wish to take account of these objections, though what I have to say may be of interest to the reader only when he is familiar with the lecture.

As to the choice of adjective, my case is simply that I could discover none that better serves my purpose. Neither "impartial," nor "disinterested," nor "impersonal," the main alternatives that I considered, seems to me as adequate in its expression; and to rest on "general," though the idea is certainly included, is to give up overtones that I intend. That those overtones are somewhat enigmatic in their content is not, from my point of view, a real deficiency; this is an enigmatic subject.

As to my meaning, I must rest upon the paper to provide the necessary exegesis, but explicit statement on one point may be of aid. In calling for neutrality of principle, I certainly do not deny that constitutional provisions are directed to protecting certain special values or that the principled development of a particular provision is concerned with the value or the values thus involved. The demand of neutrality is that a value and its measure be determined by a general analysis that gives no weight to accidents of application, finding a scope that is acceptable whatever interest, group, or person may assert the claim. So too, when there is conflict among values having constitutional protection, calling for their ordering or their accommodation, I argue that the principle of resolution must be neutral in a comparable sense (both in the definition of the individual competing values and in the approach that it entails to value competition).

Issues of federalism, for example, such as those involved in the interpretation of the commerce clause, may not be made to turn on the material interest that is affected, be it that of labor or of management, producers or consumers, or whatever other faction is at bar. The relevant principles involve abstractions about state and central government; they must do service in delineation of the governmental structure, whatever claims to power or advantage win political acceptance for the time.

Whether the Fourteenth Amendment should be read to outlaw race or color as determinants of all official action must be tested not alone by the effect of such a principle on state-required segregation but also by its impact upon measures that take race into account to equalize job opportunity or to reduce *de facto* segregation, as in New York City's schools.

The thesis is, however, so profusely illustrated in the lecture that I shall not multiply examples here.

(2) I am aware that many who agree with me in theory are not led to share my doubts about particular decisions, especially those dealing with the white primary, restrictive covenant enforcement, and public school segregation. Two of my friends at Yale have put their views in print and I commend their papers to the reader. See Louis H. Pollak, "Racial Discrimination and Judicial Integrity: A Reply to Professor Wechsler,"[1] and Charles L. Black, Jr., "The Lawfulness of the

[1] 108 U. PA. L. REV. 1 (November 1959).

Segregation Decisions."[2] It is significant for me that these defenses of the judgments advance reasons differing substantially from the opinions of the Court. They thus contribute to the inquiry I hoped to stimulate in areas where bland contentment with results has satisfied too many academic minds. I wish that I could add that I am able to accept these rationales as an answer to the difficulties I have raised. The reader is entitled to be told that I am not, but I invite him to pursue the question further and to reach an independent judgment.

(3) Since the initial publication of "The Political Safeguards of Federalism," the Senate has again considered the proposed amendment of the constitutional provisions governing election of the President. The resolution brought to the floor in 1956, with the support of the Judiciary Committee, combined the proportional division and the district systems, each of which had strong adherents. Under it a state would have been required either to divide its electoral votes in proportion to the statewide vote for the respective candidates or else to allocate one vote for the determination of the voters in each of the state's congressional districts. The unit rule that all states now are free to use and use would have been barred.

Thanks largely to Senators Douglas and Kennedy and the analysis and data they presented in their speeches, the proposal was decisively defeated. Compared to the uninformed and unperceptive discussion in 1950, when proportional division was overwhelmingly supported in the Senate, the 1956 debate represents a dramatic and significant advance. Indeed, the student who follows the thread of argument through volume 102, pt. 4 of the Congressional Record will find the best text that I know on the relation between our electoral

[2] 69 YALE L.J. 421 (January 1960).

system and the influence accorded diverse groups and sections in our politics. Some editorial writers who have been incapable of grasping the potential impact of the proportional division plan, including those of both the *New York Times* and *Washington Post-Times Herald*, would do well to give it close attention. Their leadership in matters of this kind would have been helpful in the past and may be needed in the future.

Without depreciating the scope or importance of the detail marshaled in the Senate presentations, I think that I may fairly say that all the crucial points are made and illustrated in "The Political Safeguards." I have not, therefore, thought it necessary to revise the text to refer to this new material, and have preferred to call attention to it here.

(4) If, as I hope, "Stone and the Constitution" whets the interest of the reader in the judicial career of Chief Justice Stone, he should not miss Alpheus T. Mason's authorized biography.[3] Where my assessment of Stone's views and work rests solely on the published record, aided perhaps by personal acquaintance, Professor Mason had available and used his private papers. On many of the decisions and positions I discuss, those papers add significant or interesting detail. Here too, however, I am satisfied that new material confirms and would not alter the appraisals and interpretations I propose. I have not hesitated, therefore, to republish.

[3] Harlan Fiske Stone, Pillar of the Law (1956).

PRINCIPLES, POLITICS, AND FUNDAMENTAL LAW

Selected Essays

Toward Neutral Principles of Constitutional Law

ON three occasions in the last few years Harvard has been hospitable to the discussion of that most abiding problem of our public law: the role of courts in general and the Supreme Court in particular in our constitutional tradition; their special function in the maintenance, interpretation, and development of the organic charter that provides the framework of our government, the charter that declares itself the "supreme law."

I have in mind, of course, Mr. Justice Jackson's undelivered Godkin lectures,[1] the papers and comments at the Marshall conference,[2] and Judge Learned Hand's addresses from this very rostrum but a year ago.[3] It does not depreciate these major contributions if I add that they comprise only a fragment of the serious, continuous attention that the subject is receiving here as well as elsewhere in the nation, not to speak of that less serious attention that is not without importance to

NOTE: This paper was delivered on April 7, 1959, as the Oliver Wendell Holmes Lecture at the Harvard Law School. It is reproduced without substantial change, except for the addition of the footnotes.

1 JACKSON, THE SUPREME COURT IN THE AMERICAN SYSTEM OF GOVERNMENT (1955).

2 GOVERNMENT UNDER LAW (Sutherland ed. 1956).

3 HAND, THE BILL OF RIGHTS (1958).

a university community, however uninstructive it may be. I should regard another venture on a theme so fully ventilated as a poor expression of appreciation for the hospitality accorded me, were I not persuaded that there is a point to make and an exercise to be performed that will not constitute mere reiteration; and that the point and exercise have special relevancy to the most important of our current controversies. Before I put my point and undertake the exercise it is appropriate, however, that I make clear where I stand upon the larger, underlying questions that have been considered on the previous occasions I have noted, particularly by Judge Hand last year. They have a bearing, as will be apparent, on the thesis that I mean to put before you later on.

I. The Basis of Judicial Review

Let me begin by stating that I have not the slightest doubt respecting the legitimacy of judicial review, whether the action called in question in a case which otherwise is proper for adjudication is legislative or executive, federal or state. I must address myself to this because the question was so seriously mooted by Judge Hand; and though he answered it in favor of the courts' assumption of the power of review, his answer has overtones quite different from those of the answer I would give.

Judge Hand's position was that "when the Constitution emerged from the Convention in September, 1787, the structure of the proposed government, if one looked to the text, gave no ground for inferring that the decisions of the Supreme Court, and *a fortiori* of the lower courts, were to be authoritative upon the Executive and the Legislature"; that "on the other hand it was probable, if indeed it was not certain, that without some arbiter whose decision should be final the whole system would have collapsed, for it was extremely unlikely that the Executive or the Legislature, having once decided, would yield to the contrary holding of another 'Department,' even of the courts"; that "for centuries it has been an accepted canon in interpretation of documents to interpolate into the text such provisions, though not expressed, as are essential to prevent the defeat of the venture at hand"; that it was therefore "altogether in keeping with established practice for the Supreme Court to assume an authority to keep the states, Congress, and the President within their prescribed powers"; and, finally and explicitly, that for the reason stated "it was not a lawless act to import into the Constitution such a grant of power."[4]

Though I have learned from past experience that disagreement with Judge Hand is usually nothing but the sheerest folly, I must make clear why I believe the power of the courts is grounded in the language of the Constitution and is not a mere interpolation. To do this you must let me quote the supremacy clause,[5] which is mercifully short:

> This Constitution, and the Laws of the United States which shall be made in Pursuance thereof; and all Treaties made, or which shall be made, under the Authority of the United States, shall be the supreme Law of the Land; and the Judges in every State shall be bound thereby, any Thing in the Constitution or Laws of any State to the Contrary notwithstanding.

Judge Hand concedes that under this clause "state courts would at times have to decide whether state laws and con-

[4] *Id.* at 27, 29, 14, 15, 29.

[5] U.S. CONST. art. VI, § 2.

stitutions, or even a federal statute, were in conflict with the federal constitution" but he adds that "the fact that this jurisdiction was confined to such occasions, and that it was thought necessary specifically to provide such a limited jurisdiction, looks rather against than in favor of a general jurisdiction."[6]

Are you satisfied, however, to view the supremacy clause in this way, as a grant of jurisdiction to state courts, implying a denial of the power and the duty to all others? This certainly is not its necessary meaning; it may be construed as a mandate to all of officialdom including courts, with a special and emphatic admonition that it binds the judges of the previously independent states. That the latter is the proper reading seems to me persuasive when the other relevant provisions of the Constitution are brought into view.

Article III, section 1 declares that the federal judicial power "shall be vested in one supreme Court, and in such inferior Courts as the Congress may from time to time ordain and establish." This represented, as you know, one of the major compromises of the Constitutional Convention and relegated the establishment *vel non* of lower federal courts to the discretion of the Congress.[7] None might have been established, with the consequence that, as in other federalisms, judicial work of first instance would all have been remitted to state courts.[8] Article III, section 2 goes on, however, to delineate the scope of the federal judicial power, providing

[6] HAND, *op. cit. supra* note 3, at 28.

[7] See 1 FARRAND, THE RECORDS OF THE FEDERAL CONVENTION 104–05, 119, 124–25 (1911), summarized in HART & WECHSLER, THE FEDERAL COURTS AND THE FEDERAL SYSTEM 17 (1953).

[8] See, *e.g.*, the position in Australia, described in Bailey, *The Federal Jurisdiction of State Courts*, 2 RES JUDICATAE 109 (1940); WHEARE, FEDERAL GOVERNMENT 68–72 (2d ed. 1951). The slow statutory development of federal-question jurisdiction in our lower federal courts is traced in HART & WECHSLER, *op. cit. supra* note 7, at 727–33, 1019–21, 1107–08, 1140–50.

that it "shall extend [*inter alia*] to all Cases, in Law and Equity, arising under this Constitution . . ." and, further, that the Supreme Court "shall have appellate jurisdiction" in such cases "with such Exceptions, and under such Regulations as the Congress shall make." Surely this means, as section 25 of the Judiciary Act of 1789[9] took it to mean, that if a state court passes on a constitutional issue, as the supremacy clause provides that it should, its judgment is reviewable, subject to congressional exceptions, by the Supreme Court, in which event that Court must have no less authority and duty to accord priority to constitutional provisions than the court that it reviews.[10] And such state cases might have encompassed every case in which a constitutional issue could possibly arise, since, as I have said, Congress need not and might not have exerted its authority to establish "inferior" federal courts.

If you abide with me thus far, I doubt that you will hesitate upon the final step. Is it a possible construction of the Constitution, measured strictly as Judge Hand admonishes by the test of "general purpose,"[11] that if Congress opts, as it has opted, to create a set of lower courts, those courts in cases falling within their respective jurisdictions and the Supreme Court when it passes on their judgments are less or differently constrained by the supremacy clause than are the state courts, and the Supreme Court when it reviews their judgments? Yet I cannot escape, what is for me the most astonishing conclusion, that this is the precise result of Judge Hand's reading of the text, as distinct from the interpolation he approves on other grounds.

[9] Act of Sept. 24, 1789, ch. 20, § 25, 1 Stat. 85.

[10] This too I think Judge Hand does not deny, though this concession appears only in the course of his description of the Jeffersonian position. See HAND, *op. cit. supra* note 3, at 5.

[11] *Id.* at 19.

It is true that Hamilton in the seventy-eighth *Federalist* does not mention the supremacy clause in his argument but rather urges the conclusion as implicit in the concept of a written constitution as a fundamental law and the accepted function of the courts as law interpreters. Marshall in *Marbury v. Madison* echoes these general considerations, though he also calls attention to the text, including the judiciary article, pointing only at the end to the language about supremacy, concerning which he says that it "confirms and strengthens the principle, supposed to be essential to all written constitutions, that a law repugnant to the constitution is void; and that *courts*, as well as other departments, are bound by that instrument."[12] Much might be said on this as to the style of reasoning that was deemed most persuasive when these documents were written but this would be irrelevant to my concern about the meaning that Judge Hand insists he cannot find within the words or structure of the Constitution, even with the aid of the historical material that surely points in the direction I suggest.[13]

You will not wonder now why I should be concerned about the way Judge Hand has read the text, despite his view that the judicial power was a valid importation to preserve the governmental plan. Here as elsewhere a position cannot be divorced from its supporting reasons; the reasons are, indeed, a part and most important part of the position. To demonstrate I quote Judge Hand:

> [S]ince this power is not a logical deduction from the structure of the Constitution but only a practical condition upon

[12] Marbury v. Madison, 5 U.S. (1 Cranch) 137, 180 (1803). (Emphasis in original.)

[13] See Hart & Wechsler, *op. cit. supra* note 7, at 14–16; Hart, Book Review, *Professor Crosskey and Judicial Review*, 67, Harv. L. Rev. 1456 (1954).

> its successful operation, it need not be exercised whenever a court sees, or thinks that it sees, an invasion of the Constitution. It is always a preliminary question how importunately the occasion demands an answer. It may be better to leave the issue to be worked out without authoritative solution; or perhaps the only solution available is one that the court has no adequate means to enforce.[14]

If this means that a court, in a case properly before it, is free — or should be free on any fresh view of its duty — either to adjudicate a constitutional objection to an otherwise determinative action of the legislature or executive, national or state, or to decline to do so, depending on "how importunately" it considers the occasion to demand an answer, could anything have more enormous import for the theory and the practice of review? What showing would be needed to elicit a decision? Would anything suffice short of a demonstration that judicial intervention is essential to prevent the government from foundering — the reason, you recall, for the interpolation of the power to decide? For me, as for anyone who finds the judicial power anchored in the Constitution, there is no such escape from the judicial obligation; the duty cannot be attenuated in this way.

The duty, to be sure, is not that of policing or advising legislatures or executives, nor even, as the uninstructed think, of standing as an ever-open forum for the ventilation of all grievances that draw upon the Constitution for support. It is the duty to decide the litigated case and to decide it in accordance with the law, with all that that implies as to a rigorous insistence on the satisfaction of procedural and jurisdictional requirements; the concept that Professor Freund reminds us was so fundamental in the thought and work of

[14] HAND, *op. cit. supra* note 3, at 15.

Mr. Justice Brandeis.[15] Only when the standing law, decisional or statutory, provides a remedy to vindicate the interest that demands protection against an infringement of the kind that is alleged, a law of remedies that ordinarily at least is framed in reference to rights and wrongs in general, do courts have any business asking what the Constitution may require or forbid, and only then when it is necessary for decision of the case that is at hand. How was it Marshall put the questions to be faced in *Marbury?*

> 1st. Has the applicant a right to the commission he demands?
>
> 2dly. If he has a right, and that right has been violated, do the laws of his country afford him a remedy?
>
> 3dly. If they do afford him a remedy, is it a *mandamus* issuing from this court?[16]

It was because he thought, as his opponents also thought,[17] that the Constitution had a bearing on the answers to these questions, that he claimed the right and duty to examine its commands.

As a legal system grows, the remedies that it affords substantially proliferate, a development to which the courts contribute but in which the legislature has an even larger hand.[18]

15 See Freund, On Understanding the Supreme Court 64–65 (1949); Freund, *Mr. Justice Brandeis: A Centennial Memoir*, 70 Harv. L. Rev. 769, 787–88 (1957). See also Bickel, The Unpublished Opinions of Mr. Justice Brandeis 1–20 (1957).

16 5 U.S. (1 Cranch) at 154.

17 It will be remembered that the Jeffersonian objections to the issuance of a mandamus to the Secretary rested on constitutional submissions with respect to the separation of judicial and executive authority. See 1 Warren, The Supreme Court in United States History 232 (1937); Kendall v. United States, 37 U.S. (12 Pet.) 524, 610 (1838); Lee, *The Origins of Judicial Control of Federal Executive Action*, 36 Geo. L.J. 287 (1948).

18 See, *e.g.*, *Developments in the Law — Remedies Against the United States and Its Officials*, 70 Harv. L. Rev. 827 (1957).

There has been major growth of this kind in our system[19] and I dare say there will be more, increasing correspondingly the number and variety of the occasions when a constitutional adjudication may be sought and must be made. Am I not right, however, in believing that the underlying theory of the courts' participation has not changed and that, indeed, the very multiplicity of remedies and grievances makes it increasingly important that the theory and its implications be maintained?

It is true, and I do not mean to ignore it, that the courts themselves regard some questions as "political," meaning thereby that they are not to be resolved judicially, although they involve constitutional interpretation and arise in the course of litigation. Judge Hand alluded to this doctrine which, insofar as its scope is undefined, he labeled a "stench in the nostrils of strict constructionists."[20] And Mr. Justice Frankfurter, in his great paper at the Marshall conference, avowed "disquietude that the line is often very thin between the cases in which the Court felt compelled to abstain from adjudication because of their 'political' nature, and the cases that so frequently arise in applying the concepts of 'liberty' and 'equality'."[21]

The line is thin, indeed, but I suggest that it is thinner than it needs to be or ought to be; that all the doctrine can defensibly imply is that the courts are called upon to judge whether the Constitution has committed to another agency of government the autonomous determination of the issue

19 Decisions that entail such growth do not always confront the underlying problem. See, *e.g.*, Harmon v. Brucker, 355 U.S. 579 (1958). Compare the opinion of Judge Prettyman below, 243 F.2d 613 (D.C. Cir. 1957).

20 HAND, *op. cit. supra* note 3, at 15.

21 Frankfurter, *John Marshall and the Judicial Function*, 69 HARV. L. REV. 217, 227–28 (1955), in GOVERNMENT UNDER LAW 6, 19 (Sutherland ed. 1956).

raised, a finding that itself requires an interpretation. Who, for example, would contend that the civil courts may properly review a judgment of impeachment when article I, section 3 declares that the "sole Power to try" is in the Senate? That any proper trial of an impeachment may present issues of the most important constitutional dimension, as Senator Kennedy reminds us in his moving story of the Senator whose vote saved Andrew Johnson,[22] is simply immaterial in this connection.

What is explicit in the trial of an impeachment or, to take another case, the seating or expulsion of a Senator or Representative[23] may well be found to be implicit in others. So it was held,[24] and rightly it appears to me, respecting the provision that the "United States shall guarantee to every State in this Union a Republican Form of Government. . . ." This guarantee appears, you will recall, in the same clause as does the duty to protect the states against invasion;[25] it envisages the possible employment of the military force and bears an obvious relationship to the autonomous authority of the

22 See Kennedy, Profiles in Courage 126 (1956).

23 U.S. Const. art. I, § 5 provides, "Each House shall be the Judge of the Elections, Returns and Qualifications of its own Members . . . . Each House may determine the Rules of its Proceedings, punish its Members for disorderly Behaviour, and, with the Concurrence of two thirds, expel a Member."

For a constitutional challenge to the sufficiency of primary irregularities as ground for the refusal to seat a United States Senator, see Beck, May It Please the Court 265 (1930).

24 Pacific States Tel. & Tel. Co. v. Oregon, 223 U.S. 118 (1912); Luther v. Borden, 48 U.S. (7 How.) 1, 42 (1849).

25 U.S. Const. art. IV, § 4: "The United States shall guarantee to every State in this Union a Republican Form of Government, and shall protect each of them against Invasion; and on Application of the Legislature, or of the Executive (when the Legislature cannot be convened) against domestic Violence."

Houses of Congress in seating their respective members.[26]

It also may be reasonable to conclude, or so it seems to me, though there are arguments the other way,[27] that the power of Congress to "make or alter" state regulations of the "Manner of holding Elections for Senators and Representatives,"[28] implying as it does a power to draw district lines or to prescribe the standards to be followed in defining them, excludes the courts from passing on a constitutional objection to state gerrymanders,[29] even if the Constitution can be thought to speak to this kind of inequality and the law of remedies gives disadvantaged voters legal standing to complain, which are both separate questions to be faced.[30]

If I may put my point again, I submit that in cases of the kind that I have mentioned, as in others that I do not pause to state,[31] the only proper judgment that may lead to an abstention from decision is that the Constitution has committed the determination of the issue to another agency of government than the courts. Difficult as it may be to make that judgment wisely, whatever factors may be rightly weighed in situations where the answer is not clear, what is involved is

26 *Cf.* Luther v. Borden, 48 U.S. (7 How.) 1, 42 (1849): "And when the senators and representatives of a State are admitted into the councils of the Union, the authority of the government under which they are appointed, as well as its republican character, is recognized by the proper constitutional authority."

27 See, *e.g.*, Lewis, *Legislative Apportionment and the Federal Courts*, 71 HARV. L. REV. 1057 (1958).

28 U.S. CONST. art. I, § 4.

29 See Colegrove v. Green, 328 U.S. 549, 554 (1946) (Frankfurter, J.); Professor Freund's comment in SUPREME COURT AND SUPREME LAW 46–47 (Cahn ed. 1954).

30 For an effort to face these questions, see Lewis, *supra* note 27, at 1071–98.

31 See HART & WECHSLER, *op. cit. supra* note 7, at 192–97, 207–09; POST, THE SUPREME COURT AND POLITICAL QUESTIONS (1936).

in itself an act of constitutional interpretation, to be made and judged by standards that should govern the interpretive process generally. That, I submit, is *toto caelo* different from a broad discretion to abstain or intervene.

The Supreme Court does have a discretion, to be sure, to grant or to deny review of judgments of the lower courts in situations in which the jurisdictional statute permits certiorari but does not provide for an appeal.[32] I need not say that this is an entirely different matter. The system rests upon the power that the Constitution vests in Congress to make exceptions to and regulate the Court's appellate jurisdiction; it is addressed not to the measure of judicial duty in adjudication of a case but rather to the right to a determination by the highest as distinguished from the lower courts. Even here, however, it is well worth noting that the Court by rule has defined standards for the exercise of its discretion,[33] standards framed in neutral terms, like the importance of the question or a conflict of decisions. Only the maintenance and the improvement of such standards[34] and, of course, their faithful application[35] can, I say with deference, protect the Court against the danger of the imputation of a bias favoring claims of one kind or another in the granting or denial of review.

Indeed, I will go further and assert that, necessary as it is

[32] 28 U.S.C. §§ 1254–57 (1952). The major steps in the statutory substitution of discretionary for obligatory Supreme Court review are traced in HART & WECHSLER, *op. cit. supra* note 7, at 400–03, 1313–21. The classic detailed account appears in FRANKFURTER & LANDIS, THE BUSINESS OF THE SUPREME COURT (1927).

[33] U.S. SUP. CT. R. 19.

[34] It is regrettable, in my view, that when the Court revised its rules in 1954 it determined not to attempt an improved articulation of the statement of "considerations governing review on certiorari." *But see* Wiener, *The Supreme Court's New Rules*, 68 HARV. L. REV. 20, 60–63 (1954).

[35] See, *e.g.*, Note, *Supreme Court Certiorari Policy in Cases Arising Under the FELA*, 69 HARV. L. REV. 1441 (1956).

that the Court's docket be confined to manageable size, much would be gained if the governing statutes could be revised to play a larger part in the delineation of the causes that make rightful call upon the time and energy of the Supreme Court.[36] Think of the protection it gave Marshall's court that there was no discretionary jurisdiction, with the consequence that he could say in *Cohens v. Virginia*:[37]

> It is most true that this Court will not take jurisdiction if it should not: but it is equally true, that it must take jurisdiction if it should. The judiciary cannot, as the legislature may, avoid a measure because it approaches the confines of the constitution. We cannot pass it by because it is doubtful. With whatever doubts, with whatever difficulties, a case may be attended, we must decide it, if it be brought before us. We have no more right to decline the exercise of jurisdiction which is given, than to usurp that which is not given. The one or the other would be treason to the constitution.

II. The Standards of Review

If courts cannot escape the duty of deciding whether actions of the other branches of the government are consistent with the Constitution, when a case is properly before them in the sense I have attempted to describe, you will not doubt the relevancy and importance of demanding what, if any, are the standards to be followed in interpretation. Are there, indeed, any criteria that both the Supreme Court and those who

[36] The present distribution of obligatory and discretionary jurisdiction derives largely, though not entirely, from the Judiciary Act of 1925, ch. 229, 43 Stat. 936, the architects of which were a committee of the Court. See Taft, *The Jurisdiction of the Supreme Court Under the Act of February 13, 1925*, 35 Yale L.J. 1 (1925); Frankfurter & Landis, *op. cit. supra* note 32, at 255–94. For major changes since 1925, see Hart & Wechsler, *op. cit. supra* note 7, at 1317.

[37] 19 U.S. (6 Wheat.) 264, 404 (1821).

undertake to praise or to condemn its judgments are morally and intellectually obligated to support?

Whatever you may think to be the answer, surely you agree with me that I am right to state the question as the same one for the Court and for its critics. An attack upon a judgment involves an assertion that a court should have decided otherwise than as it did. Is it not clear that the validity of an assertion of this kind depends upon assigning reasons that should have prevailed with the tribunal; and that any other reasons are irrelevant? That is, of course, not only true of a critique of a decision of the courts; it applies whenever a determination is in question, a determination that it is essential to make either way. Is it the irritation of advancing years that leads me to lament that our culture is not rich with critics who respect these limitations of the enterprise in which they are engaged?

You may remind me that, as someone in the ancient world observed — perhaps it was Josephus — history has little tolerance for any of those reasonable judgments that have turned out to be wrong. But history, in this sense, is inscrutable, concealing all its verdicts in the bosom of the future; it is never a contemporary critic.

I revert then to the problem of criteria as it arises for both courts and critics — by which I mean criteria that can be framed and tested as an exercise of reason and not merely as an act of willfulness or will. Even to put the problem is, of course, to raise an issue no less old than our culture. Those who perceive in law only the element of fiat, in whose conception of the legal cosmos reason has no meaning or no place, will not join gladly in the search for standards of the kind I have in mind. I must, in short, expect dissent *in limine* from anyone whose view of the judicial process leaves no room for the antinomy Professor Fuller has so gracefully explored.[38] So too must I anticipate dissent from those more numerous among us who, vouching no philosophy to warranty, frankly or covertly make the test of virtue in interpretation whether its result in the immediate decision seems to hinder or advance the interests or the values they support.

I shall not try to overcome the philosophic doubt that I have mentioned, although to use a phrase that Holmes so often used — "it hits me where I live." That battle must be fought on wider fronts than that of constitutional interpretation; and I do not delude myself that I can qualify for a command, great as is my wish to render service. The man who simply lets his judgment turn on the immediate result may not, however, realize that his position implies that the courts are free to function as a naked power organ, that it is an empty affirmation to regard them, as ambivalently he so often does, as courts of law. If he may know he disapproves of a decision when all he knows is that it has sustained a claim put forward by a labor union or a taxpayer, a Negro or a segregationist, a corporation or a Communist — he acquiesces in the proposition that a man of different sympathy but equal information may no less properly conclude that he approves.

You will not charge me with exaggeration if I say that this type of *ad hoc* evaluation is, as it has always been, the deepest problem of our constitutionalism, not only with respect to judgments of the courts but also in the wider realm in which conflicting constitutional positions have played a part in our politics.

Did not New England challenge the embargo that the South

[38] See Fuller, *Reason and Fiat in Case Law*, 59 HARV. L. REV. 376 (1946).

supported on the very ground on which the South was to resist New England's demand for a protective tariff?[39] Was not Jefferson in the Louisiana Purchase forced to rest on an expansive reading of the clauses granting national authority of the very kind that he had steadfastly opposed in his attacks upon the Bank?[40] Can you square his disappointment about Burr's acquittal on the treason charge and his subsequent request for legislation[41] with the attitude towards freedom and

[39] See 4 ADAMS, HISTORY OF THE UNITED STATES OF AMERICA DURING THE SECOND ADMINISTRATION OF THOMAS JEFFERSON 267 (1890): "If Congress had the right to regulate commerce for such a purpose in 1808, South Carolina seemed to have no excuse for questioning, twenty years later, the constitutionality of a protective system."

[40] See 2 ADAMS, HISTORY OF THE UNITED STATES OF AMERICA DURING THE FIRST ADMINISTRATION OF THOMAS JEFFERSON 90 (1889): "[T]he Louisiana treaty gave a fatal wound to 'strict construction,' and the Jeffersonian theories never again received general support. In thus giving them up, Jefferson did not lead the way, but he allowed his friends to drag him in the path they chose." See also 3 WILSON, A HISTORY OF THE AMERICAN PEOPLE 182–83 (1902).

[41] In his annual message of October 27, 1807, Jefferson said: "I shall think it my duty to lay before you the proceedings and the evidence publicly exhibited on the arraignment of the principal offenders before the circuit court of Virginia. You will be enabled to judge whether the defect was in the testimony, in the law, or in the administration of the law; and wherever it shall be found, the Legislature alone can apply or originate the remedy. The framers of our Constitution certainly supposed that they had guarded as well their Government against destruction by treason as their citizens against oppression under pretense of it, and if these ends are not attained it is of importance to inquire by what means more effectual they may be secured," 1 RICHARDSON, MESSAGES AND PAPERS OF THE PRESIDENT 429 (1896). The trial proceedings were transmitted to the Senate on November 23, 1807. See 17 ANNALS OF CONG. APP. 385–778 (1807).

Jefferson's conception of the "remedy" not only involved legislation overcoming Marshall's strict construction of the treason clause but also a provision for the removal of judges on the address of both Houses of Congress. See 3 RANDALL, THE LIFE OF THOMAS JEFFERSON 246–47 (1865); 1 WARREN, THE SUPREME COURT IN UNITED STATES HISTORY 311–15 (1937).

On the former point, different bills were introduced in the Senate and the House. The Senate bill by Giles undertook to define "levying war" for purposes of treason. The proposed definition included "assembling them-

repression most enduringly associated with his name? Were the abolitionists who rescued fugitives and were acquitted in defiance of the evidence able to distinguish their view of the compulsion of a law of the United States from that advanced by South Carolina in the ordinance that they despised?[42]

To bring the matter even more directly home, what shall we think of the Harvard records of the Class of 1829, the class of Mr. Justice Curtis, which, we are told,[43] praised at length the Justice's dissent in the *Dred Scott* case but then added, "Again, *and seemingly adverse to the above*, in October, 1862, he prepared a legal opinion and argument, which was published in Boston in pamphlet form, to the effect that President Lincoln's Proclamation of prospective emancipation of the slaves in the rebellious States is *unconstitutional*."

Of course, a man who thought and, as a Justice, voted and maintained[44] that a free Negro could be a citizen of the United States and therefore of a state, within the meaning of the constitutional and statutory clauses defining the diversity jurisdiction; that Congress had authority to forbid slavery within a territory, even one acquired after the formation of the Union; and that such a prohibition worked emancipation of a slave whose owner brought him to reside in such a territory —

---

selves together with intent forcibly to overturn or change the Government of the United States, or any one of the Territories thereof . . . or forcibly to resist the general execution of any public law thereof . . . or if any person or persons shall traitorously aid or assist in the doing any of the acts aforesaid, although not personally present when any such act is done . . . ." 17 ANNALS OF CONG. 108–09 (1808). For discussion of the measure in the Senate, see 17 *id.* at 109–27, 135–49. The House bill by Randolph defined a separate offense, "conspiracy to commit treason against the United States . . . ." 18 *id.* at 1717–18.

42 See South Carolina Ordinance of Nullification, 1 S.C. Stat. 329 (1832).

43 See 1 CURTIS, A MEMOIR OF BENJAMIN ROBBINS CURTIS 354–55 n.1 (1879).

44 See Scott v. Sandford, 60 U.S. (19 How.) 393, 564–633 (1857).

a man who thought all these things detracted obviously from the force of his positions if he also thought the President without authority to abrogate a form of property established and protected by state law within the states where it was located, states which the President and his critic alike maintained had not effectively seceded from the Union and were not a foreign enemy at war.

How simple the class historian could make it all by treating as the only thing that mattered whether Mr. Justice Curtis had, on the occasions noted, helped or hindered the attainment of the freedom of the slaves.

I have cited these examples from the early years of our history since time has bred aloofness that may give them added force. What a wealth of illustration is at hand today! How many of the constitutional attacks upon congressional investigations of suspected Communists have their authors felt obliged to launch against the inquiries respecting the activities of Goldfine or of Hoffa or of others I might name? How often have those who think the Smith Act, as construed, inconsistent with the first amendment made clear that they also stand for constitutional immunity for racial agitators fanning flames of prejudice and discontent? Turning the case around, are those who in relation to the Smith Act see no virtue in distinguishing between advocacy of merely abstract doctrine and advocacy which is planned to instigate unlawful action,[45] equally unable to see virtue in the same distinction in relation, let us say, to advocacy of resistance to the judgments of the courts, especially perhaps to judgments vindicating claims that equal protection of the laws has been denied? I may live a uniquely sheltered life but am I wrong in thinking I discerned in some extremely warm enthusiasts for jury trial a certain diminution of enthusiasm as the issue was presented in

[45] See Yates v. United States, 354 U.S. 298, 318 (1957).

the course of the debate in 1957 on the bill to extend federal protection of our civil rights?

All I have said, you may reply, is something no one will deny, that principles are largely instrumental as they are employed in politics, instrumental in relation to results that a controlling sentiment demands at any given time. Politicians recognize this fact of life and are obliged to trim and shape their speech and votes accordingly, unless perchance they are prepared to step aside; and the example that John Quincy Adams set somehow is rarely followed.

That is, indeed, all I have said but I now add that whether you are tolerant, perhaps more tolerant than I, of the *ad hoc* in politics, with principle reduced to a manipulative tool, are you not also ready to agree that something else is called for from the courts? I put it to you that the main constituent of the judicial process is precisely that it must be genuinely principled, resting with respect to every step that is involved in reaching judgment on analysis and reasons quite transcending the immediate result that is achieved. To be sure, the courts decide, or should decide, only the case they have before them. But must they not decide on grounds of adequate neutrality and generality, tested not only by the instant application but by others that the principles imply? Is it not the very essence of judicial method to insist upon attending to such other cases, preferably those involving an opposing interest, in evaluating any principle avowed?

Here too I do not think that I am stating any novel or momentous insight. But now, as Holmes said long ago in speaking of "the unrest which seems to wonder vaguely whether law and order pay," we "need education in the obvious."[46] We need it more particularly now respecting constitutional

[46] HOLMES, *Law and the Court*, in COLLECTED LEGAL PAPERS 291, 292 (1920).

interpretation, since it has become a commonplace to grant what many for so long denied: that courts in constitutional determinations face issues that are inescapably "political" — political in the third sense that I have used that word — in that they involve a choice among competing values or desires, a choice reflected in the legislative or executive action in question, which the court must either condemn or condone.

I should be the last to argue otherwise or to protest the emphasis upon the point in Mr. Justice Jackson's book, throughout the Marshall conference, and in the lectures by Judge Hand. I have, indeed, insisted on the point myself.[47] But what is crucial, I submit, is not the nature of the question but the nature of the answer that may validly be given by the courts. No legislature or executive is obligated by the nature of its function to support its choice of values by the type of reasoned explanation that I have suggested is intrinsic to judicial action — however much we may admire such a reasoned exposition when we find it in those other realms.

Does not the special duty of the courts to judge by neutral principles addressed to all the issues make it inapposite to contend, as Judge Hand does, that no court can review the legislative choice — by any standard other than a fixed "historical meaning" of constitutional provisions[48] — without becoming "a third legislative chamber"?[49] Is there not, in short, a vital difference between legislative freedom to appraise the gains and losses in projected measures and the kind of principled appraisal, in respect of values that can reasonably be asserted to have constitutional dimension, that alone is in the province of the courts? Does not the difference yield a middle ground

[47] See, *e.g.*, Wechsler, *Comment* on Snee, *Leviathan at the Bar of Justice*, in Government Under Law 134, 136–37 (Sutherland ed. 1956).

[48] Hand, *op. cit. supra* note 3, at 65.

[49] *Id.* at 42.

between a judicial House of Lords and the abandonment of any limitation on the other branches — a middle ground consisting of judicial action that embodies what are surely the main qualities of law, its generality and its neutrality? This must, it seems to me, have been in Mr. Justice Jackson's mind when in his chapter on the Supreme Court "as a political institution" he wrote[50] in words that I find stirring, "Liberty is not the mere absence of restraint, it is not a spontaneous product of majority rule, it is not achieved merely by lifting underprivileged classes to power, nor is it the inevitable by-product of technological expansion. It is achieved only by a rule of law." Is it not also what Mr. Justice Frankfurter must mean in calling upon judges for "allegiance to nothing except the effort, amid tangled words and limited insights, to find the path through precedent, through policy, through history, to the best judgment that fallible creatures can reach in that most difficult of all tasks: the achievement of justice between man and man, between man and state, through reason called law"?[51]

You will not understand my emphasis upon the role of reason and of principle in the judicial, as distinguished from the legislative or executive, appraisal of conflicting values to imply that I depreciate the duty of fidelity to the text of the Constitution, when its words may be decisive — though I would certainly remind you of the caution stated by Chief Justice Hughes: "Behind the words of the constitutional provisions are postulates which limit and control."[52] Nor will you take me to deny that history has weight in the elucidation

[50] JACKSON, THE SUPREME COURT IN THE AMERICAN SYSTEM OF GOVERNMENT 76 (1955).

[51] FRANKFURTER, *Chief Justices I Have Known*, in OF LAW AND MEN 138 (Elman ed. 1956).

[52] Principality of Monaco v. Mississippi, 292 U.S. 313, 322 (1934).

of the text, though it is surely subtle business to appraise it as a guide. Nor will you even think that I deem precedent without importance, for we surely must agree with Holmes that "imitation of the past, until we have a clear reason for change, no more needs justification than appetite."[53] But after all, it was Chief Justice Taney who declared his willingness "that it be regarded hereafter as the law of this court, that its opinion upon the construction of the Constitution is always open to discussion when it is supposed to have been founded in error, and that its judicial authority should hereafter depend altogether on the force of the reasoning by which it is supported."[54] Would any of us have it otherwise, given the nature of the problems that confront the courts?

At all events, is not the relative compulsion of the language of the Constitution, of history and precedent — where they do not combine to make an answer clear — itself a matter to be judged, so far as possible, by neutral principles — by standards that transcend the case at hand? I know, of course, that it is common to distinguish, as Judge Hand did, clauses like "due process," cast "in such sweeping terms that their history does not elucidate their contents,"[55] from other provisions of the Bill of Rights addressed to more specific problems. But the contrast, as it seems to me, often implies an overstatement of the specificity or the immutability these other clauses really have — at least when problems under them arise.

No one would argue, for example, that there need not be indictment and a jury trial in prosecutions for a felony in district courts. What made a question of some difficulty was

[53] HOLMES, *Holdsworth's English Law*, in COLLECTED LEGAL PAPERS 285, 290 (1920).

[54] Passenger Cases, 48 U.S. (7 How.) 283, 470 (1849).

[55] HAND, *op. cit. supra* note 3, at 30.

the issue whether service wives charged with the murders of their husbands overseas could be tried there before a military court.[56] Does the language of the double-jeopardy clause or its preconstitutional history actually help to decide whether a defendant tried for murder in the first degree and convicted of murder in the second, who wins a reversal of the judgment on appeal, may be tried again for murder in the first or only murder in the second?[57] Is there significance in the fact that it is "jeopardy of life or limb" that is forbidden, now that no one is in jeopardy of limb but only of imprisonment or fine? The right to "have the assistance of counsel" was considered, I am sure, when the sixth amendment was proposed, a right to defend by counsel if you have one, contrary to what was then the English law.[58] That does not seem to me sufficient to avert extension of its meaning to imply a right to court-appointed counsel when the defendant is too poor to find such aid[59] — though I admit that I once urged the point sincerely as a lawyer for the Government.[60] It is difficult for me to think the fourth amendment freezes for all time the common law of search and of arrest as it prevailed when the amendment was adopted, whatever the exigencies of police problems may now be or may become. Nor should we, in my view, lament the fact that "the" freedom of speech or press that Congress is forbidden by the first amendment to impair is not determined

56 See Reid v. Covert, 354 U.S. 1 (1957), *reversing on rehearing* 351 U.S. 487 (1956).

57 See Green v. United States, 355 U.S. 184 (1957).

58 "Throughout the eighteenth century counsel were allowed to speak in cases of treason and misdemeanour only." 1 STEPHEN, A HISTORY OF THE CRIMINAL LAW OF ENGLAND 453 (1883). See also ASSOCIATION OF THE BAR OF THE CITY OF NEW YORK & NATIONAL LEGAL AID & DEFENDER ASS'N, EQUAL JUSTICE FOR THE ACCUSED 40–42 (1959).

59 See Johnson v. Zerbst, 304 U.S. 458 (1938).

60 Walker v. Johnston, 312 U.S. 275 (1941).

only by the scope such freedom had in the late eighteenth century, though the word "the" might have been taken to impose a limitation to the concept of that time — a time when, President Wright has recently reminded us, there was remarkable consensus about matters of this kind.[61]

Even "due process," on the other hand, might have been confined, as Mr. Justice Brandeis urged originally,[62] to a guarantee of fair procedure, coupled perhaps with prohibition of executive displacement of established law — the analogue for us of what the barons meant in Magna Carta. Equal protection could be taken as no more than an assurance that no one may be placed beyond the safeguards of the law, outlawing, as it were, the possibility of outlawry, but nothing else. Here too I cannot find it in my heart to regret that interpretation did not ground itself in ancient history but rather has perceived in these provisions a compendious affirmation of the basic values of a free society, values that must be given weight in legislation and administration at the risk of courting trouble in the courts.

So far as possible, to finish with my point, I argue that we should prefer to see the other clauses of the Bill of Rights read as an affirmation of the special values they embody rather than as statements of a finite rule of law, its limits fixed by the consensus of a century long past, with problems very different from our own. To read them in the former way is to leave

61 WRIGHT, CONSENSUS AND CONTINUITY, 1776–1787 *passim* (1958). See also CHAFEE, HOW HUMAN RIGHTS GOT INTO THE CONSTITUTION (1952). For the suggestion that political consensus has been the abiding characteristic of American democracy, see HARTZ, THE LIBERAL TRADITION IN AMERICA 139–42 (1955).

62 "Despite arguments to the contrary which had seemed to me persuasive, it is settled that the due process clause of the Fourteenth Amendment applies to matters of substantive law as well as to matters of procedure." Whitney v. California, 274 U.S. 357, 373 (1927) (concurring opinion).

room for adaptation and adjustment if and when competing values, also having constitutional dimension, enter on the scene.

Let me repeat what I have thus far tried to say. The courts have both the title and the duty when a case is properly before them to review the actions of the other branches in the light of constitutional provisions, even though the action involves value choices, as invariably action does. In doing so, however, they are bound to function otherwise than as a naked power organ; they participate as courts of law. This calls for facing how determinations of this kind can be asserted to have any legal quality. The answer, I suggest, inheres primarily in that they are — or are obliged to be — entirely principled. A principled decision, in the sense I have in mind, is one that rests on reasons with respect to all the issues in the case, reasons that in their generality and their neutrality transcend any immediate result that is involved. When no sufficient reasons of this kind can be assigned for overturning value choices of the other branches of the Government or of a state, those choices must, of course, survive. Otherwise, as Holmes said in his first opinion for the Court, "a constitution, instead of embodying only relatively fundamental rules of right, as generally understood by all English-speaking communities, would become the partisan of a particular set of ethical or economical opinions . . ."[63]

The virtue or demerit of a judgment turns, therefore, entirely on the reasons that support it and their adequacy to maintain any choice of values it decrees, or, it is vital that we add, to maintain the rejection of a claim that any given choice should be decreed. The critic's role, as T. R. Powell showed throughout so many fruitful years, is the sustained, disinterested, merciless examination of the reasons that the courts ad-

[63] Otis v. Parker, 187 U.S. 606, 609 (1903).

vance, measured by standards of the kind I have attempted to describe. I wish that more of us today could imitate his dedication to that task.

III. Some Appraisals of Review

One who has ventured to advance such generalities about the courts and constitutional interpretation is surely challenged to apply them to some concrete problems — if only to make clear that he believes in what he says. A lecture, to be sure, is a poor medium for such an undertaking, for the statement and analysis of cases inescapably takes time. Nonetheless, I feel obliged to make the effort and I trust that I can do so without trespassing on the indulgence you already have displayed.

Needless to say, I must rely on you to understand that in alluding to some areas of constitutional interpretation, selected for their relevancy to my thesis, I do not mean to add another capsulated estimate of the performance of our highest court to those that now are in such full supply. The Court in constitutional adjudications faces what must surely be the largest and the hardest task of principled decision-making faced by any group of men in the entire world. There is a difference worthy of articulation between purported evaluations of the Court and comments on decisions or opinions.

(1) I start by noting two important fields of present interest in which the Court has been decreeing value choices in a way that makes it quite impossible to speak of principled determinations or the statement and evaluation of judicial reasons, since the Court has not disclosed the grounds on which its judgments rest.

The first of these involves the sequel to the *Burstyn* case,[64]

[64] Joseph Burstyn, Inc. v. Wilson, 343 U.S. 495 (1952).

in which, as you recall, the Court decided that the motion picture is a medium of expression included in the "speech" and "press" to which the safeguards of the first amendment, made applicable to the states by the fourteenth, apply. But *Burstyn* left open, as it was of course obliged to do, the extent of the protection that the movies are accorded, and even the question whether any censorship is valid, involving as it does prior restraint. The judgment rested, and quite properly, upon the vice inherent in suppression based upon a finding that the film involved was "sacrilegious" — with the breadth and vagueness that that term had been accorded in New York. "[W]hether a state may censor motion pictures under a clearly drawn statute designed and applied to prevent the showing of obscene films" was said to be "a very different question" not decided by the Court.[65] In five succeeding cases, decisions sustaining censorship of different films under standards variously framed have been reversed, but only by per curiam decisions. In one of these,[66] in which I should avow I was of counsel, the standard was undoubtedly too vague for any argument upon the merits. I find it hard to think that this was clearly so in all the others.[67] Given the subtlety and difficulty of the problem, the need and opportunity for clarifying explanation, are such unexplained decisions in a new

65 *Id.* at 506.

66 Gelling v. Texas, 343 U.S. 960, *reversing per curiam* 157 Tex. Crim. 516, 247 S.W.2d 95 (1952) (ordinance prohibited exhibition of picture deemed by Censorship Board "of such character as to be prejudicial to the best interests of the people" of Marshall, Texas, "if publicly shown").

67 See Times Film Corp. v. City of Chicago, 355 U.S. 35, *reversing per curiam* 244 F.2d 432 (7th Cir. 1957); Holmby Prods., Inc. v. Vaughn, 350 U.S. 870, *reversing per curiam* 177 Kan. 728, 282 P.2d 412 (1955); Superior Films, Inc. v. Department of Educ., 346 U.S. 587 (1954), *reversing per curiam* 159 Ohio St. 315, 112 N.E.2d 311 (1953); Superior Films, Inc. v. Department of Educ., *supra, reversing per curiam* Commercial Pictures Corp. v. Board of Regents of the Univ. of N.Y., 305 N.Y. 336, 113 N.E.2d 502 (1953).

domain of constitutional interpretation consonant with standards of judicial action that the Court or we can possibly defend? I realize that nine men often find it easier to reach agreement on result than upon reasons and that such a difficulty may be posed within this field. Is it not preferable, however, indeed essential, that if this is so the variations of position be disclosed?[68]

The second group of cases to which I shall call attention involves what may be called the progeny of the school-segregation ruling of 1954. Here again the Court has written on the merits of the constitutional issue posed by state segregation only once;[69] its subsequent opinions on the form of the decree[70] and the defiance in Arkansas[71] deal, of course, with other matters. The original opinion, you recall, was firmly focused on state segregation in the public schools, its reason-

[68] Attention should be called to Kingsley Int'l Pictures Corp. v. Regents of the Univ. of N.Y., 360 U.S. 684 (1959), decided with full opinions since the present paper was delivered. The Court was unanimous in holding invalid New York's refusal to license the exhibition of a film based on D. H. Lawrence's *Lady Chatterley's Lover*. The opinion of the Court by Mr. Justice Stewart, deeming the censorship order to rest solely on the ground that the picture portrays an adulterous relationship as an acceptable pattern of behavior, held the statute so construed an unconstitutional impairment of freedom to disseminate ideas. Justices Black and Douglas joined in the opinion but in brief concurrences expressed their view that any prior restraint on motion pictures is as vulnerable as the censorship of newspapers or books. Mr. Justice Frankfurter in one opinion and Mr. Justice Harlan in another, joined by Justices Frankfurter and Whittaker, conceived of the New York statute as demanding some showing of obscenity or of incitement to immorality and thought, therefore, that it escaped the condemnation of the majority opinion. In their view, however, the film could not be held to have embodied either obscenity or incitement. Hence, the statute was invalid as applied.

[69] Brown v. Board of Educ., 347 U.S. 483 (1954). See also Bolling v. Sharpe, 347 U.S. 497 (1954), dealing with segregation in the District of Columbia.

[70] Brown v. Board of Educ., 349 U.S. 294 (1955).

[71] Cooper v. Aaron, 358 U.S. 1 (1958).

ing accorded import to the nature of the educational process, and its conclusion was that separate educational facilities are "inherently unequal."

What shall we think then of the Court's extension of the ruling to other public facilities, such as public transportation, parks, golf courses, bath houses, and beaches, which no one is obliged to use — all by per curiam decisions?[72] That these situations present a weaker case against state segregation is not, of course, what I am saying. I am saying that the question whether it is stronger, weaker, or of equal weight appears to me to call for principled decision. I do not know, and I submit you cannot know, whether the per curiam affirmance in the *Dawson* case, involving public bath houses and beaches, embraced the broad opinion of the circuit court that all state-enforced racial segregation is invalid or approved only its immediate result and, if the latter, on what ground. Is this "process of law," to borrow the words Professor Brown has used so pointedly in writing of such unexplained decisions upon matters far more technical[73] — the process that alone affords the Court its title and its duty to adjudicate a claim that state action is repugnant to the Constitution?

Were I a prudent man I would, no doubt, confine myself to problems of this order, involving not the substance but the method of decision — for other illustrations might be cited in

[72] New Orleans City Park Improvement Ass'n v. Detiege, 358 U.S. 54, *affirming per curiam* 252 F.2d 122 (5th Cir. 1958); Gayle v. Browder, 352 U.S. 903, *affirming per curiam* 142 F. Supp. 707 (M.D. Ala. 1956); Holmes v. City of Atlanta, 350 U.S. 879, *reversing per curiam* 223 F.2d 93 (5th Cir. 1955); Mayor & City Council v. Dawson, 350 U.S. 877, *affirming per curiam* 220 F.2d 386 (4th Cir. 1955); Muir v. Louisville Park Theatrical Ass'n, 347 U.S. 971 (1954), *reversing per curiam* 202 F.2d 275 (6th Cir. 1953).

[73] Brown, *Foreword: Process of Law, The Supreme Court, 1957 Term,* 72 HARV. L. REV. 77 (1958).

the same domain. I shall, however, pass beyond this to some areas of substantive interpretation which appear to me to illustrate my theme.

(2) The phase of our modern constitutional development that I conceive we can most confidently deem successful inheres in the broad reading of the commerce, taxing, and related powers of the Congress, achieved with so much difficulty little more than twenty years ago — against restrictions in the name of state autonomy to which the Court had for a time turned such a sympathetic ear.

Why is it that the Court failed so completely in the effort to contain the scope of national authority and that today one reads decisions like *Hammer v. Dagenhart*,[74] or *Carter Coal*,[75] or the invalidation of the Agricultural Adjustment Act[76] with eyes that disbelieve? No doubt the answer inheres partly in the simple facts of life and the consensus they have generated on the powers that a modern nation needs. But is it not a feature of the case as well — a feature that has real importance — that the Court could not articulate an adequate analysis of the restrictions it imposed on Congress in favor of the states, whose representatives — upon an equal footing in the Senate — controlled the legislative process and had broadly acquiesced in the enactments that were subject to review?

Is it not also true and of importance that some of the principles the Court affirmed were strikingly deficient in neutrality, sustaining, for example, national authority when it impinged adversely upon labor, as in the application of the Sherman Act, but not when it was sought to be employed in labor's aid? On this score, the contrast in today's position cer-

[74] 247 U.S. 251 (1918).
[75] Carter v. Carter Coal Co., 298 U.S. 238 (1936).
[76] United States v. Butler, 297 U.S. 1 (1936).

tainly is striking. The power that sustained the Wagner Act is the same power that sustains Taft-Hartley — with its even greater inroads upon state autonomy but with restraints on labor that the Wagner Act did not impose.

One of the speculations that I must confess I find intriguing is upon the question whether there are any neutral principles that might have been employed to mark the limits of the commerce power of the Congress in terms more circumscribed than the virtual abandonment of limits in the principle that has prevailed. Given the readiness of President Roosevelt to compromise on any basis that allowed achievement of the substance of his program, might not the formulae of coverage employed in the legislation of the thirties have quite readily embraced any such principles the Court had then been able to devise before the crisis became so intense — principles sustaining action fairly equal to the need? I do not say we would or should be happier if that had happened and the Court still played a larger part within this area of our federalism, given the attention to state interests that is so inherent in the Congress and the constitutional provisions governing the selection and the composition of the Houses, which make that attention very likely to endure.[77] I say only that I find such speculation interesting. You will recall that it was Holmes who deprecated argument of counsel the logic of which left "no part of the conduct of life with which on similar principles Congress might not interfere."[78]

(3) The poverty of principled articulation of the limits put on Congress as against the states before the doctrinal reversal of the thirties was surely also true of the decisions, deal-

77 For further development of this point, see pp. 54–64, *infra*.

78 Northern Sec. Co. v. United States, 193 U.S. 197, 403 (1904) (dissenting opinion).

ing with the very different problem of the relation between the individual and government, which invoked due process to maintain *laissez faire*. Did not the power of the great dissents inhere precisely in their demonstrations that the Court could not present an adequate analysis, in terms of neutral principles, to support the value choices it decreed? Holmes, to be sure, saw limits beyond which "the contract and due process clauses are gone"; and his insistence on the need for compensation to sustain a Pennsylvania prohibition of the exploitation of subsurface coal, threatening subsidence of a dwelling belonging to the owner of the surface land, indicates the kind of limit he perceived.[79] Am I simply voicing my own sympathies in saying that his analysis of those limits has a thrust entirely lacking in the old and now forgotten judgments striking down minimum-wage and maximum-hour laws?

If I am right in this it helps to make a further point that has more bearing upon current issues, that I believe it misconceives the problem of the Court to state it as the question of the proper measure of judicial self-restraint, with the resulting issue whether such restraint is only proper in relation to protection of a purely economic interest or also in relation to an interest like freedom of speech or of religion, privacy, or discrimination (at least if it is based on race, origin, or creed). Of course, the courts ought to be cautious to impose a choice of values on the other branches or a state, based upon the Constitution, only when they are persuaded, on an adequate and principled analysis, that the choice is clear. That I suggest is all that self-restraint can mean and in that sense it always is essential, whatever issue may be posed. The real test inheres, as I have tried to argue, in the force of the analysis. Surely a stronger analysis may be advanced against a particular un-

[79] Pennsylvania Coal Co. v. Mahon, 260 U.S. 393, 412 (1922).

compensated taking as a violation of the fifth amendment than against a particular limitation of freedom of speech or press as a violation of the first.

In this view, the "preferred position" controversy hardly has a point — indeed, it never has been really clear what is asserted or denied to have a preference and over what.[80] Certainly the concept is pernicious if it implies that there is any simple, almost mechanistic basis for determining priorities of values having constitutional dimension, as when there is an inescapable conflict between claims to free press and a fair trial. It has a virtue, on the other hand, insofar as it recognizes that some ordering of social values is essential; that all cannot be given equal weight, if the Bill of Rights is to be maintained.

Did Holmes mean any less than this when he lamented the tendency "toward underrating or forgetting the safeguards in bills of rights that had to be fought for in their day and that still are worth fighting for"?[81] Only in that view could he have dissented in the *Abrams* and the *Gitlow* cases[82] and have struggled so intensely to develop a principled delineation of the freedom that he voted to sustain. Even if one thinks, as I confess I do, that his analysis does not succeed if it requires that an utterance designed to stimulate unlawful action must be accorded an immunity unless it is intended to achieve or creates substantial danger of *immediate* results,[83] can anyone

80 See, *e.g.*, Kovacs v. Cooper, 336 U.S. 77, 88 (1949).

81 2 HOLMES-POLLOCK LETTERS 25 (Howe ed. 1941); see 1 HOLMES-LASKI LETTERS 203, 529–30 (Howe ed. 1953); *cf.* 2 *id.* at 888.

82 Abrams v. United States, 250 U.S. 616, 624 (1919); Gitlow v. New York, 268 U.S. 652, 672 (1925).

83 "I do not doubt for a moment that by the same reasoning that would justify punishing persuasion to murder, the United States constitutionally may punish speech that produces or is intended to produce a clear and imminent danger that it will bring about forthwith certain substantive evils that the United States constitutionally may seek to prevent." Abrams v.

deny it his respect? Is not the force of a position framed in terms of principles of the neutrality and generality that Holmes achieved entirely different from that of the main opinion, for example, in the *Sweezy* case,[84] resting at bottom as it does, on principles of power separation among the branches of state government that never heretofore have been conceived to be a federal requirement and that, we safely may predict, the Court will not apply to any other field?[85]

(4) Finally, I turn to the decisions that for me provide the hardest test of my belief in principled adjudication, some of those in which the Court in recent years has vindicated claims that deprivations based on race deny the equality before the law that the fourteenth amendment guarantees. The crucial cases are, of course, those involving the white primary,[86] the enforcement of racially restrictive covenants,[87] and the segregated schools.[88]

The more I think about the past the more skeptical I find myself about predictions of the future. Viewed a priori would you not have thought that the invention of the cotton gin in 1792 should have reduced the need for slave labor and hence

United States, 250 U.S. 616, 627 (1919). Is it possible, however, that persuasion to murder is only punishable constitutionally if the design is that the murder be committed "forthwith"? *Cf.* HAND, *op. cit. supra* note 3, at 58–59.

84 Sweezy v. New Hampshire, 354 U.S. 234 (1957).

85 See Uphaus v. Wyman, 360 U.S. 72, 77 (1959), decided after the present paper was delivered: "[S]ince questions concerning the authority of the committee to act as it did are questions of state law, . . . we accept as controlling the New Hampshire Supreme Court's conclusion that '[t]he legislative history makes it clear beyond a reasonable doubt that it [the Legislature] did and does desire an answer to these questions'."

86 Smith v. Allwright, 321 U.S. 649 (1944).

87 Shelley v. Kraemer, 334 U.S. 1 (1948); Barrows v. Jackson, 346 U.S. 249 (1953).

88 Brown v. Board of Educ., 347 U.S. 483 (1954).

diminished the attractiveness of slavery? Brooks Adams tells us that its consequences were precisely the reverse; that the demand for slaves increased as cotton planting became highly lucrative, increased so greatly that Virginia turned from coal and iron, which George Washington envisaged as its future, into an enormous farm for breeding slaves — forty thousand of whom it exported annually to the rest of the South.[89] Only the other day I read that the Japanese evacuation, which I thought an abomination when it happened, though in the line of duty as a lawyer I participated in the effort to sustain it in the Court,[90] is now believed by many to have been a blessing to its victims, breaking down forever the ghettos in which they had previously lived.[91] But skeptical about predictions as I am, I still believe that the decisions I have mentioned — dealing with the primary, the covenant, and schools — have the best chance of making an enduring contribution to the quality of our society of any that I know in recent years. It is in this perspective that I ask how far they rest on neutral principles and are entitled to approval in the only terms that I acknowledge to be relevant to a decision of the courts.

The primary and covenant cases present two different aspects of a single problem — that it is a state alone that is forbidden by the fourteenth amendment to deny equal protection of the laws, as only a state or the United States is precluded by the fifteenth amendment from denying or abridging on the ground of race or color the right of citizens of the United States to vote. It has, of course, been held for years that the prohibition of action by the state reaches not only an

[89] See B. Adams, *The Heritage of Henry Adams*, in H. ADAMS, THE DEGRADATION OF THE DEMOCRATIC DOGMA 22, 31 (1919).

[90] Korematsu v. United States, 323 U.S. 214 (1944).

[91] See Newsweek, Dec. 29, 1958, p. 23.

explicit deprivation by a statute but also action of the courts or of subordinate officials, purporting to exert authority derived from public office.[92]

I deal first with the primary. So long as the Democratic Party in the South excluded Negroes from participation, in the exercise of an authority conferred by statute regulating political parties, it was entirely clear that the amendment was infringed; the exclusion involved an application of the statute.[93] The problem became difficult only when the states, responding to these judgments, repealed the statutes, leaving parties free to define their membership as private associations, protected by the state but not directed or controlled or authorized by law. In this position the Court held in 1935 that an exclusion by the party was untouched by the amendment, being action of the individuals involved, not of the state or its officialdom.[94]

Then came the *Classic* case[95] in 1941, which I perhaps should say I argued for the Government. *Classic* involved a prosecution of election officials for depriving a voter of a right secured by the Constitution in willfully failing to count his vote as it was cast in a Louisiana Democratic primary. In holding that the right of a qualified voter to participate in choosing Representatives in Congress, a right conferred by article I, section 2,[96] extended to participating in a primary which influenced the ultimate selection, the Court did not, of

[92] See, *e.g.*, *Ex parte* Virginia, 100 U.S. 339, 347 (1880); Hale, Freedom Through Law ch. xi (1952).

[93] See Nixon v. Condon, 286 U.S. 73 (1932); Nixon v. Herndon, 273 U.S. 536 (1927).

[94] Grovey v. Townsend, 295 U.S. 45 (1935).

[95] United States v. Classic, 313 U.S. 299 (1941).

[96] "The House of Representatives shall be composed of Members chosen every second Year by the People of the several States, and the Electors in each State shall have the Qualifications requisite for Electors of the most numerous Branch of the State Legislature."

course, deal with the scope of party freedom to select its members. The victim of the fraud in *Classic* was a member of the Democratic Party, voting in a primary in which he was entitled to participate, and the only one in which he could.[97] Yet three years later *Classic* was declared in *Smith v. Allwright*[98] to have determined in effect that primaries are a part of the election, with the consequence that parties can no more defend racial exclusion from their primaries than can the state, a result reaffirmed in 1953.[99] This is no doubt a settled proposition in the Court. But what it means is not, as sometimes has been thought, that a state may not escape the limitations of the Constitution merely by transferring public functions into private hands. It means rather that the constitutional guarantee against deprivation of the franchise on the ground of race or color has become a prohibition of party organization upon racial lines, at least where the party has achieved political hegemony. I ask with all sincerity if you are able to

The seventeenth amendment contains similar provisions for the choice of Senators.

97 The Government brief in *Classic* stated with respect to *Grovey:* "Moreover, what Article I, Section 2 secures is the right to choose. The implicit premise of the *Grovey* decision is that the negroes excluded from the Democratic primary were legally free to record their choice by joining an opposition party or by organizing themselves. In the present case the voters exercised the right to choose in accordance with the contemplated method; and the wrong alleged deprived them of an opportunity to express their choice in any other way." Brief for the United States, pp. 34–35, United States v. Classic, 313 U.S. 299 (1941).

98 321 U.S. 649 (1944). Mr. Justice Frankfurter concurred only in the result. Mr. Justice Roberts alone dissented.

99 Terry v. Adams, 345 U.S. 461 (1953). See also Rice v. Elmore, 165 F.2d 387 (4th Cir. 1947), *cert. denied,* 333 U.S. 875 (1948). There is no opinion of the Court in *Terry.* Justices Douglas and Burton joined in an opinion by Justice Black. Justice Frankfurter, saying that he found the case "by no means free of difficulty," wrote for himself. Chief Justice Vinson and Justices Reed and Jackson joined in an opinion by Justice Clark. Justice Minton dissented.

discover in the opinions thus far written in support of this result — a result I say again that I approve — neutral principles that satisfy the mind. I should suppose that a denial of the franchise on religious grounds is certainly forbidden by the Constitution. Are religious parties, therefore, to be taken as proscribed? I should regard this result too as one plainly to be desired but is there a constitutional analysis on which it can be validly decreed? Is it, indeed, not easier to project an analysis establishing that such a proscription would infringe rights protected by the first amendment?

The case of the restrictive covenant presents for me an even harder problem. Assuming that the Constitution speaks to state discrimination on the ground of race but not to such discrimination by an individual even in the use or distribution of his property, although his freedom may no doubt be limited by common law or statute, why is the enforcement of the private covenant a state discrimination rather than a legal recognition of the freedom of the individual? That the action of the state court is action of the state, the point Mr. Chief Justice Vinson emphasizes in the Court's opinion[100] is, of course, entirely obvious. What is not obvious, and is the crucial step, is that the state may properly be charged with the discrimination when it does no more than give effect to an agreement that the individual involved is, by hypothesis, entirely free to make. Again, one is obliged to ask: What is the principle involved? Is the state forbidden to effectuate a will that draws a racial line, a will that can accomplish any disposition only through the aid of law, or is it a sufficient answer there that the discrimination was the testator's and not the state's?[101] May not the state employ its law to vindicate

[100] See Shelley v. Kraemer, 334 U.S. 1, 14–23 (1948).

[101] *Cf.* Gordon v. Gordon, 332 Mass. 197, 210, 124 N.E.2d 228, 236, *cert. denied*, 349 U.S. 947 (1955).

the privacy of property against a trespasser, regardless of the grounds of his exclusion, or does it embrace the owner's reasons for excluding if it buttresses his power by the law? Would a declaratory judgment that a fee is determinable if a racially restrictive limitation should be violated represent discrimination by the state upon the racial ground?[102] Would a judgment of ejectment?

None of these questions has been answered by the Court nor are the problems faced in the opinions.[103] Philadelphia, to be sure, has been told that it may not continue to administer the school for "poor male white orphans," established by the city as trustee under the will of Stephen Girard, in accordance with that racial limitation.[104] All the Supreme Court said, however, was the following: "The Board which operates Girard College is an agency of the State of Pennsylvania. Therefore, even though the Board was acting as a trustee, its refusal to admit Foust and Felder to the college because they were Negroes was discrimination by the State. Such discrimination is forbidden by the Fourteenth Amendment." When the Orphans' Court thereafter dismissed the city as trustee, appointing individuals in substitution, its action was sustained in Pennsylvania.[105] Further review by certiorari was denied.[106]

One other case in the Supreme Court has afforded opportunity for reconsidering the basis and scope of the *Shelley*

[102] See Charlotte Park & Recreation Comm'n v. Barringer, 242 N.C. 311, 88 S.E.2d 114 (1955), *cert. denied*, 350 U.S. 983 (1956).

[103] Mr. Chief Justice Vinson, dissenting in Barrows v. Jackson, 346 U.S. 249, 260 (1953), urged a distinction between enforcement of the covenant by injunction, the problem in *Shelley*, and an action for damages against a defaulting covenantor by a co-covenantor. He was alone in his dissent.

[104] Pennsylvania v. Board of Directors, 353 U.S. 230, 231 (1957).

[105] Girard College Trusteeship, 391 Pa. 434, 441-42, 138 A.2d 844, 846 (1958).

[106] Pennsylvania v. Board of Directors, 357 U.S. 570 (1958).

principle, *Black v. Cutter Labs.*[107] Here a collective-bargaining agreement was so construed that Communist Party membership was "just cause" for a discharge. In this view, California held that a worker was lawfully dismissed upon that ground. A Supreme Court majority concluded that this judgment involved nothing but interpretation of a contract, making irrelevant the standards that would govern the validity of a state statute that required the discharge. Only Mr. Chief Justice Warren and Justices Douglas and Black, dissenting, thought the principle of *Shelley v. Kraemer* was involved when the state court sustained the discharge.[108]

Many understandably would like to perceive in the primary and covenant decisions a principle susceptible of broad extension, applying to the other power aggregates in our society limitations of the kind the Constitution has imposed on government.[109] My colleague A. A. Berle, Jr., has, indeed, pointed to the large business corporation, which after all is chartered by the state and wields in many areas more power than the government, as uniquely suitable for choice as the next subject of such application.[110] I doubt that the courts will yield to such temptations; and I do not hesitate to say that I prefer to

[107] 351 U.S. 292 (1956).

[108] Attention also should be called to Dorsey v. Stuyvesant Town Corp., 299 N.Y. 512, 87 N.E.2d 541 (1949), holding state action not involved in racial discrimination in the selection of tenants by the owner corporation, although the housing development involved had been constructed with the aid of New York City which, pursuant to a contract authorized by statute, had condemned the land for the corporation and granted substantial tax exemptions. Certiorari was denied, 339 U.S. 981 (1950), Justices Black and Douglas noting their dissent.

[109] See, *e.g.*, Ming, *Racial Restrictions and the Fourteenth Amendment: The Restrictive Covenant Cases*, 16 U. Chi. L. Rev. 203, 235–38 (1949).

[110] See, *e.g.*, Berle, *Constitutional Limitations on Corporate Activity — Protection of Personal Rights From Invasion Through Economic Power*, 100 U. Pa. L. Rev. 933, 948–51 (1952); Berle, Economic Power and Free Society 17–18 (Fund for the Republic 1957).

see the issues faced through legislation, where there is room for drawing lines that courts are not equipped to draw. If this is right the two decisions I have mentioned will remain, as they now are, *ad hoc* determinations of their narrow problems, yielding no neutral principles for their extension or support.

Lastly, I come to the school decision, which for one of my persuasion stirs the deepest conflict I experience in testing the thesis I propose. Yet I would surely be engaged in playing Hamlet without Hamlet if I did not try to state the problems that appear to me to be involved.

The problem for me, I hardly need to say, is not that the Court departed from its earlier decisions holding or implying that the equality of public educational facilities demanded by the Constitution could be met by separate schools. I stand with the long tradition of the Court that previous decisions must be subject to reexamination when a case against their reasoning is made. Nor is the problem that the Court disturbed the settled patterns of a portion of the country; even that must be accepted as a lesser evil than nullification of the Constitution. Nor is it that history does not confirm that an agreed purpose of the fourteenth amendment was to forbid separate schools or that there is important evidence that many thought the contrary;[111] the words are general and leave room for expanding content as time passes and conditions change. Nor is it that the Court may have miscalculated the extent to which its judgment would be honored or accepted; it is not a prophet of the strength of our national commitment to respect the judgments of the courts. Nor is it even that the Court did not remit the issue to the Congress, acting under the

111 See Bickel, *The Original Understanding and the Segregation Decision*, 69 HARV. L. REV. 1 (1955).

enforcement clause of the amendment. That was a possible solution, to be sure, but certainly Professor Freund is right[112] that it would merely have evaded the claims made.

The problem inheres strictly in the reasoning of the opinion, an opinion which is often read with less fidelity by those who praise it than by those by whom it is condemned. The Court did not declare, as many wish it had, that the fourteenth amendment forbids all racial lines in legislation, though subsequent per curiam decisions may, as I have said, now go that far. Rather, as Judge Hand observed,[113] the separate-but-equal formula was not overruled "in form" but was held to have "no place" in public education on the ground that segregated schools are "inherently unequal," with deleterious effects upon the colored children in implying their inferiority, effects which retard their educational and mental development. So, indeed, the district court had found as a fact in the Kansas case, a finding which the Supreme Court embraced, citing some further "modern authority" in its support.[114]

Does the validity of the decision turn then on the sufficiency of evidence or of judicial notice to sustain a finding that the separation harms the Negro children who may be involved? There were, indeed, some witnesses who expressed that opinion in the Kansas case,[115] as there were also witnesses in the companion Virginia case, including Professor Garrett of Columbia,[116] whose view was to the contrary. Much de-

[112] See Freund, *Storm Over the American Supreme Court*, 21 MODERN L. REV. 345, 351 (1958).

[113] HAND, *op. cit. supra* note 3, at 54.

[114] For a detailed account of the character and quality of research in this field, see Note, *Grade School Segregation: The Latest Attack on Racial Discrimination*, 61 YALE L.J. 730 (1952).

[115] See Record, pp. 125–26, 132 (Hugh W. Speer), Brown v. Board of Educ., 347 U.S. 483 (1954); *id.* at 164–65 (Wilbur B. Brookover); *id.* at 170–71 (Louisa Holt); *id.* at 176–79 (John J. Kane).

[116] See Record, pp. 548–55, 568–72 (Henry E. Garrett), Davis v. County Bd. of Educ., 347 U.S. 483 (1954).

pended on the question that the witness had in mind, which rarely was explicit. Was he comparing the position of the Negro child in a segregated school with his position in an integrated school where he was happily accepted and regarded by the whites; or was he comparing his position under separation with that under integration where the whites were hostile to his presence and found ways to make their feelings known? And if the harm that segregation worked was relevant, what of the benefits that it entailed: sense of security, the absence of hostility? Were they irrelevant? Moreover, was the finding in Topeka applicable without more to Clarendon County, South Carolina, with 2799 colored students and only 295 whites? Suppose that more Negroes in a community preferred separation than opposed it? Would that be relevant to whether they were hurt or aided by segregation as opposed to integration? Their fates would be governed by the change of system quite as fully as those of the students who complained.

I find it hard to think the judgment really turned upon the facts. Rather, it seems to me, it must have rested on the view that racial segregation is, in principle, a denial of equality to the minority against whom it is directed; that is, the group that is not dominant politically and, therefore, does not make the choice involved. For many who support the Court's decision this assuredly is the decisive ground. But this position also presents problems. Does it not involve an inquiry into the motive of the legislature, which is generally foreclosed to the courts?[117] Is it alternatively defensible to make the measure of validity of legislation the way it is interpreted by those

[117] Motive is open to examination when executive action is challenged as discriminatory, but there the purpose is to show that an admitted inequality of treatment was not inadvertent. See, *e.g.*, Snowden v. Hughes, 321 U.S. 1 (1944). Even in such a case, invidious motivation alone has not been held to establish the inequality.

who are affected by it? In the context of a charge that segregation *with equal facilities* is a denial of equality, is there not a point in *Plessy* in the statement that if "enforced separation stamps the colored race with a badge of inferiority" it is solely because its members choose "to put that construction upon it"?[118] Does enforced separation of the sexes discriminate against females merely because it may be the females who resent it and it is imposed by judgments predominantly male? Is a prohibition of miscegenation a discrimination against the colored member of the couple who would like to marry?

For me, assuming equal facilities, the question posed by state-enforced segregation is not one of discrimination at all. Its human and its constitutional dimensions lie entirely elsewhere, in the denial by the state of freedom to associate, a denial that impinges in the same way on any groups or races that may be involved. I think, and I hope not without foundation, that the Southern white also pays heavily for segregation, not only in the sense of guilt that he must carry but also in the benefits he is denied. In the days when I was joined with Charles H. Houston in a litigation in the Supreme Court, before the present building was constructed, he did not suffer more than I in knowing that we had to go to Union Station to lunch together during the recess. Does not the problem of miscegenation show most clearly that it is the freedom of association that at bottom is involved, the only case, I may add, where it is implicit in the situation that association is desired by the only individuals involved? I take no pride in knowing that in 1956 the Supreme Court dismissed an appeal in a case in which Virginia nullified a marriage on this ground, a case in which the statute had been squarely challenged by the de-

[118] Plessy v. Ferguson, 163 U.S. 537, 551 (1896).

fendant, and the Court, after remanding once, dismissed per curiam on procedural grounds that I make bold to say are wholly without basis in the law.[119]

But if the freedom of association is denied by segregation, integration forces an association upon those for whom it is unpleasant or repugnant. Is this not the heart of the issue involved, a conflict in human claims of high dimension, not unlike many others that involve the highest freedoms — conflicts that Professor Sutherland has recently described.[120] Given a situation where the state must practically choose between denying the association to those individuals who wish it or imposing it on those who would avoid it, is there a basis in neutral principles for holding that the Constitution demands that the claims for association should prevail? I should like to think there is, but I confess that I have not yet written the opinion. To write it is for me the challenge of the school-segregation cases.

Having said what I have said, I certainly should add that I offer no comfort to anyone who claims legitimacy in defiance of the courts. This is the ultimate negation of all neutral principles, to take the benefits accorded by the constitutional system, including the national market and common defense, while denying it allegiance when a special burden is imposed. That certainly is the antithesis of law.

I am confident I have said much with which you disagree — both in my basic premises and in conclusions I have drawn. The most that I can hope is that the effort be considered worthy of a rostrum dedicated to the memory of Mr. Justice

[119] See Ham Say Naim v. Naim, 197 Va. 80, 87 S.E.2d 749, *vacated*, 350 U.S. 891 (1955), *on remand*, 197 Va. 734, 90 S.E.2d 849, *appeal dismissed*, 350 U.S. 985 (1956).

[120] See SUTHERLAND, THE LAW AND ONE MAN AMONG MANY 35–62 (1956).

Holmes. Transcending all the lessons that he teaches through the years, the most important one for me has come to this: Those of us to whom it is not given to "live greatly in the law" are surely called upon to fail in the attempt.

The Political Safeguards of Federalism

The Role of the States in the Composition and Selection of the National Government

FEDERALISM was the means and price of the formation of the Union. It was inevitable, therefore, that its basic concepts should determine much of our history. The more important fact is that they shape government, law, and politics today. Nor is this merely illustration of the insight that the lives of nations, like the lives of individuals, are permanently influenced by the experience of infancy. In a far flung, free society, the federalist values are enduring. They call upon a people to

NOTE: This is in major part a paper submitted to the Conference on Federalism held January 11–14, 1954, in connection with the Bicentennial Celebration of Columbia University. See FEDERALISM—MATURE AND EMERGENT (MacMahon ed. 1955). It also includes material drawn from *Presidential Elections and the Constitution,* 35 A.B.A.J. 181 (1949).

achieve a unity sufficient to resist their common perils and advance their common welfare, without undue sacrifice of their diversities and the creative energies to which diversity gives rise. They call for government responsive to the will of the full national constituency, without loss of responsiveness to lesser voices, reflecting smaller bodies of opinion, in areas that constitute their own legitimate concern.

No form of government can serve these values with complete efficiency, no set of mechanisms can perfectly discriminate between the polar claims so patently involved. No single form or mechanism will give equal service under different circumstances or function with the same results at different times. But in a time when federalism must appear to many peoples as the sole alternative to tyranny, there is a special value in examining American experience, the more so since we face important issues of direction ourselves.

I

Our constitution makers established a central government authorized to act directly upon individuals through its own agencies — and thus they formed a nation capable of function and of growth. To serve the ends of federalism they employed three main devices: (1) They preserved the states as separate sources of authority and organs of administration — a point on which they hardly had a choice. (2) They gave the states a role of great importance in the composition and selection of the central government. (3) They undertook to formulate a distribution of authority between the nation and the states, in terms which gave some scope at least to legal processes for its enforcement.

Scholarship — not only legal scholarship — has given most

attention to the last of these enumerated mechanisms, perhaps because it has been fascinated by the Supreme Court and its interpretations of the power distribution clauses of the Constitution. The continuous existence of the states as governmental entities and their strategic role in the selection of the Congress and the President are so immutable a feature of the system that their importance tends to be ignored. Of the framers' mechanisms, however, they have had and have today the larger influence upon the working balance of our federalism. The actual extent of central intervention in the governance of our affairs is determined far less by the formal power distribution than by the sheer existence of the states and their political power to influence the action of the national authority.

The fact of the continuous existence of the states, with general governmental competence unless excluded by the Constitution or valid Act of Congress, set the mood of our federalism from the start. The first Congress did not face the problem of building a legal system from the ground up; it started with the premise that the standing *corpus juris* of the country was provided by the states. As with the law, so with the courts. One federal Supreme Court was essential and the Constitution gave a mandate that it be established. But even the establishment of lower courts was left an open question by the framers, as was the jurisdiction to be vested in any such courts as Congress might establish — within the limits that the Constitution set. Congress was free to commit the administration of national law to national tribunals or to leave the task to the state courts, sworn to support the national supremacy within its proper sphere.[1] Even the appellate juris-

[1] For Justice Story's view that Congress was obliged to vest full jurisdiction over federal matters in a federal court either originally or on appeal,

diction of the Supreme Court was subject to congressional control.

National action has thus always been regarded as exceptional in our polity, an intrusion to be justified by some necessity, the special rather than the ordinary case. This point of view cuts even deeper than the concept of the central government as one of granted, limited authority, articulated in the tenth amendment. National power may be quite unquestioned in a given situation; those who would advocate its exercise must none the less answer the preliminary question why the matter should not be left to the states. Even when Congress acts, its tendency has been to frame enactments on an *ad hoc* basis to accomplish limited objectives, supplanting state-created norms only so far as may be necessary for the purpose. Indeed, with all the centralizing growth throughout the years, federal law is still a largely interstitial product, rarely occupying any field completely, building normally upon legal relationships established by the states. As Henry Hart and I have put it elsewhere: "Congress acts . . . against the background of the total *corpus juris* of the states in much the way that a state legislature acts against the background of the common law, assumed to govern unless changed by legislation."[2] As a state

see Martin v. Hunter's Lessee, 14 U.S. (1 Wheat.) 304, 328 (1816); 3 STORY, COMMENTARIES ON THE CONSTITUTION 449 (1833). The position was recently supported by Professor Crosskey. See 1 CROSSKEY, POLITICS AND THE CONSTITUTION IN THE HISTORY OF THE UNITED STATES 612 *et seq.* (1953). It seems, however, to be plainly contrary to the purport of one of the major compromises of the Constitutional Convention. See HART & WECHSLER, THE FEDERAL COURTS AND THE FEDERAL SYSTEM 17–18 (1953). It was, of course, rejected by the Congress in the framing of the Judiciary Act of 1789 and the rejection has prevailed. See Warren, *New Light on the History of the Federal Judiciary Act of 1789*, 37 HARV. L. REV. 49, 65 (1923); Hart, *The Relations Between State and Federal Law*, 54 COLUM. L. REV. 489, 501–02 (1954).

[2] HART & WECHSLER, *op. cit. supra* note 1, at 435.

legislature views the common law as something to be left alone unless a need for change has been established, so Congress has traditionally viewed the governance of matters by the states.

The tradition plainly serves the values of our federalism in so far as it maintains a burden of persuasion on those favoring national intervention. New York, for example, faced the need for rent control after the need was deemed to have passed in most parts of the country. Should a national program have been continued when New York and every other state was competent to launch a program of its own, adapted to its special needs? Under such circumstances national action has consequences that are plainly undesirable. On the one hand, it is likely to impose control in areas where the politically dominant local judgment finds control unnecessary. On the other hand, it is likely to attenuate the rigor of control in areas where it is really needed. For if the need is not severe the country over, the terms of national legislation will be shaped by a Congress in which the hostile sentiment has a large influence, rather than by a legislature more generally sensitive to the need. This was, of course, the actual experience with federal control of rent throughout the later postwar years.[3]

The political logic of federalism thus supports placing the burden of persuasion on those urging national action. Though the explanation is the same, it is more difficult to find support

[3] On the dissatisfaction in New York with the progressive relaxation of federal rent control, culminating in the substitution of state control pursuant to the "local option" provision of the federal act of 1949, 63 STAT. 18, 26 (1949), 50 U.S.C. APP. § 1894(j) (Supp. 1952), see Teeval Co. v. Stern, 301 N.Y. 346, 93 N.E.2d 884 (1950); TEMPORARY CITY HOUSING RENT COMMISSION, CONTROL OF EVICTIONS AND OF RESIDENTIAL RENTS BY NEW YORK CITY (1950); REPORT OF N.Y. STATE TEMPORARY COMMISSION TO STUDY RENTS AND RENTAL CONDITIONS, N.Y. LEG. DOC. No. 49 (1950); Wechsler, *Next Steps in Rent Control*, 5 THE RECORD 126 (1950).

for the commonly fragmentary quality of many national enactments, with their resultant ambiguity as to how far they supersede state law entirely and how far they call for integration with it. This is a point that has a special visibility to lawyers, for the federal-state adjustments called for by such ambiguities present problems of enormous difficulty to the courts.[4] The issue is perhaps most striking in the common case where federal law defines powers, rights, or duties without attention to resulting liabilities or remedies, raising the question whether these are matters to be governed by state legal systems or determined by the independent judgment of federal courts.[5] To explore these matters is beyond my present purpose. I adduce them only to support my thesis that the existence of the states as governmental entities and as the sources of the standing law is in itself the prime determinant of our working federalism, coloring the nature and the scope of our national legislative processes from their inception.

II

If I have drawn too much significance from the mere fact of the existence of the states, the error surely will be rectified by pointing also to their crucial role in the selection and the composition of the national authority. More is involved here than that aspect of the compromise between the larger and the smaller states that yielded their equality of status in the Senate.

[4] Taft-Hartley is a good example. See, *e.g.*, Garner v. Teamsters Union, 346 U.S. 485 (1953); Hart, *supra* note 1, at 526–36. The problems of federalism in labor relations were fully considered at the Conference by Paul R. Hays in his paper, *Federalism and Labor Relations in the United States*, 102 U. PA. L. REV. 959 (1954).

[5] See Hart, *supra* note 1, at 523–24, 529–30, 534–35; Wechsler, *Federal Jurisdiction and the Revision of the Judicial Code*, 13 LAW & CONTEMP. PROB. 216, 241 (1948).

Representatives no less than Senators are allotted by the Constitution to the states, although their number varies with state population as determined by the census. Though the House was meant to be the "grand depository of the democratic principle of the government,"[6] as distinguished from the Senate's function as the forum of the states, the people to be represented with due deference to their respective numbers were *the people of the states.* And with the President, as with Congress, the crucial instrument of the selection — whether through electors, or, in the event of failure of majority, by the House voting as state units — is again the states. The consequence, of course, is that the states are the strategic yardsticks for the measurement of interest and opinion, the special centers of political activity, the separate geographical determinants of national as well as local politics.

Despite the rise of national parties, the shift to popular election of the Senate and the difficulty of appraising the precise impact of such provisions on the legislative process, Madison's analysis has never lost its thrust:

> The State governments may be regarded as constituent and essential parts of the federal government; whilst the latter is nowise essential to the operation or organization of the former.[7]
>
> A local spirit will infallibly prevail much more in the members of Congress, than a national spirit will prevail in the legislatures of the particular States.[8]
>
> Even the House of Representatives, though drawn immediately from the people, will be chosen very much under the influence of that class of men, whose influence over the

[6] George Mason in the Convention, 5 Elliot's Debates 136 (1876).
[7] The Federalist, No. 45 at 288 (Lodge ed. 1888).
[8] *Id.*, No. 46 at 294.

people obtains for themselves an election into the State legislatures.[9]

To the extent that federalist values have real significance they must give rise to local sensitivity to central intervention; to the extent that such a local sensitivity exists, it cannot fail to find reflection in the Congress.[10] Indeed, the problem of the Congress is and always has been to attune itself to national opinion and produce majorities for action called for by the voice of the entire nation. It is remarkable that it should function thus as well as it does, given its intrinsic sensitivity to any insular opinion that is dominant in a substantial number of the states.

III

The point is so clear in the Senate that, as Madison observed of the equality accorded to the states, it "does not call for much discussion."[11] Prior to the admission of Alaska and Hawaii, the forty-nine votes that would determine Senate action, even with full voting, could theoretically have been drawn from twenty-five states, of which the combined population did not reach twenty-nine millions, a bare nineteen per cent of all state residents.[12] The one-third plus one that would

[9] *Id.*, No. 45 at 288–89.

[10] Many members of Congress have, of course, served previously in state government. For an analysis of the prior state service of the Senate in the Eightieth Congress, including twenty-eight former governors, see HOLCOMBE, OUR MORE PERFECT UNION 205–06 (1950).

[11] THE FEDERALIST, No. 62 at 385 (Lodge ed. 1888).

[12] The states referred to and their populations (according to the 1950 census) are:

Arizona	749,587	Idaho	588,637
Arkansas	1,909,511	Kansas	1,905,299
Colorado	1,325,089	Maine	913,774
Connecticut	2,007,280	Mississippi	2,178,914
Delaware	318,085	Montana	591,024

defeat a treaty or a resolution of amendment could, equally theoretically, have been drawn from seventeen states with a total population little over twelve millions, less than that of New York. I say theoretically since, short of a combination to resist an effort to impair state equality within the Senate (which the Constitution purports to place beyond amendment) or to diminish the political power of the smaller states in other ways, a coalition in these terms is quite unthinkable. The fact remains that in more subtle ways the Senate cannot fail to function as the guardian of state interests as such, when they are real enough to have political support or even to be instrumental in attaining other ends. And if account is taken of the operation of seniority within the Senate, of the opportunity of Senators to marshal individual authority, not to speak of the possibility of filibuster, this power of negation, vested in the states without regard to population, multiplies in many ways. Given a controversy that has any sectional dimension, it is not long before the impact of this power is perceived.[18]

Nor is it only power of negation. To be sure, on any direct show of strength in passing legislation, a Senate majority based

Nebraska	1,325,510	South Carolina	2,117,027
Nevada	160,083	South Dakota	652,740
New Hampshire	533,242	Utah	688,862
New Mexico	681,187	Vermont	377,747
North Dakota	619,636	Washington	2,378,963
Oklahoma	2,233,351	West Virginia	2,005,552
Oregon	1,521,341	Wyoming	290,529
Rhode Island	791,896		

The apportionment allotted these states 86 Representatives in a House of 435.

[18] Any judicious estimate upon this point must take account of Lindsay Rogers' thesis that, sectional controversies apart, the Senate has traditionally taken a much broader and disinterested view of public questions than the House. See Rogers, The American Senate (1926), especially ch. iv.

on the states must be supported by a House majority based on population and must also avoid a veto by the President. But power to enact is rarely based on such a test — and when it seems to be, there sometimes is involved a merely token process. Legislation rests in practice on a balancing of interests, a give and take that calls for coalition and for compromise, a strategy that may involve a present sacrifice to hold or win future support.[14] In this dynamic interchange, a latent power of negation has much positive significance in garnering the votes for an enactment that might otherwise have failed. This is the point at which state equality may well present the largest difficulties, but the issue is beyond the range I have undertaken to explore. It is enough for present purposes to show how far the composition of the Senate is intrinsically calculated to prevent intrusion from the center on subjects that dominant state interests wish preserved for state control.

IV

Even the House is slanted somewhat in the same direction, though the incidence is less severe. This is not due appreciably to the one seat reserved for every state regardless of its population, nor to the mechanics or the mathematics of congressional apportionment, though they present their problems.[15] It is due rather to the states' control of voters' qualifications, on the one hand, and of districting, on the other.

The position with respect to voters' qualifications derives from the constitutional provision that fixes the electorate of Representatives (and of Senators as well since the seventeenth

[14] See, *e.g.*, Fischer, *Unwritten Rules of American Politics*, 197 HARPER'S 27 (1948); HOLCOMBE, OUR MORE PERFECT UNION 208–10 (1950); GROSS, THE LEGISLATIVE STRUGGLE (1953), especially at 148–50.

[15] See SCHMECKEBIER, CONGRESSIONAL APPORTIONMENT (1941); Schmeckebier, *The Method of Equal Proportions*, 17 LAW & CONTEMP. PROB. 302 (1952); Willcox, *Last Words on the Apportionment Problem*, 17 *id.* at 290.

amendment) as those persons who "have the qualifications requisite for electors of the most numerous branch of the State Legislature."[16] Subject, then, to the prohibition of the denial of franchise because of color, race, or sex, embodied in the fifteenth and nineteenth amendments and the radiations of the equal protection clause of the fourteenth, the states determine — indirectly it is true — the electorate that chooses Representatives.[17] The consequences of contracting the electorate by such devices as a poll tax are, of course, incalculable, but they tend to buttress what traditionally dominant state interests conceive to be their special state position; that is the point of the contraction. This sentiment, reflected in the Representatives that these constituencies send to Congress, is not ordinarily conducive to support for an adventurous expansion of the national authority, though there have been exceptions, to be sure.

The fourteenth amendment purports to put in the hands of Congress a remedy for such diminution of the electorate. It directs that the census figure determinative of the number of a state's representatives be reduced on the apportionment to the extent that the right to vote "is denied to any of the male inhabitants of such state, being twenty-one years of age and citizens of the United States, or in any way abridged, except for participation in rebellion, or other crime." The remedy has proved unworkable in practice by reason of the difficulty of the quantitative investigation needed,[18] not to speak of the political problems that an effort to employ it would present.

16 U.S. CONST. art. I, § 2.

17 See United States v. Classic, 313 U.S. 299, 314–15 (1941).

18 See SCHMECKEBIER, CONGRESSIONAL APPORTIONMENT 94–96 (1941). See also *id.* at 97 *et seq.* for the suggestion that the purpose of the unenforceable provision of the fourteenth amendment should be achieved by a further amendment basing the apportionment of representatives on the number of votes cast in a state rather than on population.

Federal abolition of the poll tax is periodically urged in Congress, with extensive hearings on the measure, but there are grave doubts with respect to its constitutionality and no real prospect of its passage.[19]

State control of congressional districting derives from the constitutional provision that the "times, places, and manner of holding elections for Senators and Representatives, shall be prescribed in each State by the Legislature thereof."[20] The same clause provides, however, that "Congress may at any time by law make or alter such regulations. . . ." Though the matter has been disputed, it seems plain that state control thus rests entirely on the tolerance of Congress.[21] Until congressional action was taken in 1842, there was variation in state practice. Alabama, Georgia, Mississippi, Missouri, New Hampshire, New Jersey, and Pennsylvania elected Representatives on a state-wide basis by general ticket, while Maryland, Massachusetts, New York, Virginia, and South Carolina were committed early to the district basis. The Act of 1842

[19] See the testimony of Charles Warren, expressing hostility to the poll tax but also opposing the constitutionality of federal abolition even in federal elections. *Hearings before Committee on House Administration on H.R. 29*, 80th Cong., 2d Sess. 145–162 (1948). Both Judiciary Committees have consistently reported in support of abolition. See, *e.g.*, SEN. REP. No. 1225, 80th Cong., 2d Sess. (1948); H.R. REP. No. 947, 80th Cong., 1st Sess. (1947). Though the measure has passed the House by overwhelming votes, see, *e.g.*, 89 CONG. REC. 4889 (1943), it has not been brought to a decision in the Senate. Compare the curiously different voting in the House on the war-time proposal to facilitate the vote of service personnel by distribution of a federal ballot, which, despite reliance on the war powers of Congress, was opposed on constitutional grounds. See 90 CONG. REC. 1229–30 (1944). Is it too cynical to suggest that voting on the poll tax abolition bills was partly influenced by knowledge that they were foredoomed to failure in the Senate?

[20] Art. I, § 4.

[21] For an excellent account see Paschal, *The House of Representatives: "Grand Depository of the Democratic Principle"?*, 17 LAW & CONTEMP. PROB. 276 (1952).

made districts "composed of contiguous territory" mandatory, though leaving districting to the respective states.[22] Even this mandate was initially defied in four of the general-ticket states, with the House seating their elected Representatives despite the state's recalcitrance as to the method of selection. Omitted in 1850, the mandate was repeated in later Acts and was extended in 1872 to require that the districts contain "as nearly as practicable an equal number of inhabitants."[23] The requirement of contiguity was further supplemented in 1901 to call for districts of "compact territory."[24] These provisions were repeated in 1911[25] but the Congress failed to reapportion after the census of 1920. The legislation of 1929, as amended,[26] establishing the present framework, provides for an automatic reapportionment upon the President's report (unless Congress directs otherwise). It directs the course that must be followed in the election of Representatives when a change from prior methods is required by an alteration of their number as a consequence of the apportionment and the state has failed to prescribe what the change shall be.[27] Beyond this, however, it lays down no requirements at all. The district system thus rests wholly upon state initiative at the present time. More important, the delineation of the districts rests entirely with the states.

It is well known that there are great discrepancies in district size in many multidistrict states, paralleling for Congress the discrepancies, to forego harsher terms, that prevail in districting for the state legislatures.[28] One study estimated that in

[22] 5 STAT. 491 (1842). [23] 17 STAT. 28 (1872).

[24] 31 STAT. 733–34 (1901). [25] 37 STAT. 13 (1911).

[26] 46 STAT. 26 (1929), as amended, 55 STAT. 761 (1941), 2 U.S.C. § 2a (1946).

[27] *Id.* § 2a(c).

[28] See HURST, THE GROWTH OF AMERICAN LAW 41–43 (1950); Harvey,

the spring of 1952, 115 of the 435 congressional districts showed variation as to size larger than fifteen per cent above or below the state average, the maximum above the average being 129.8 per cent in Texas and, below the average, 51.3 per cent in South Dakota (where there are only two districts).[29] Writing before redistricting occurred in some fifteen states, Professor Holcombe's committee of the American Political Science Association said:

> The Committee has noted with concern the great disparities in the 1950 populations of existing Congressional districts. Take 350,000 as roughly the average in a district. In one state, there is a district under 175,000; six others under 250,000; three between 500,000 and 700,000, and one exceeding 900,000. In many states, the spread between 1950 population in the smallest and the largest existing district in the State is two or three hundred thousand.[30]

The committee proposed a remedy which was in turn proposed to Congress by President Truman in his message of January 9, 1951, reporting the reapportionment.[31] The main features were these: (1) that Congress restore the earlier requirement of single-member districts composed of contiguous and compact territory and containing as nearly as practicable the same number of inhabitants; (2) that it forbid deviations in excess of 50,000 above or below the norm of 350,000 per-

---

Reapportionment of State Legislatures—Legal Requirements, 17 LAW & CONTEMP. PROB. 364 (1952); Shell, *Political and Partisan Implications of State Legislative Apportionment,* 17 *id.* at 417.

[29] See Todd, *The Apportionment Problem Faced by the States,* 17 *id.* at 314, 337 (1952).

[30] *The Reapportionment of Congress,* 45 AM. POL. SCI. REV. 153, 154 (1951).

[31] 97 CONG. REC. 114 (1951).

sons to a district; (3) that Congress itself take measures to eliminate a larger variation, even to prescribing the redistricting in cases where the state persists in deviating from the standard thus laid down. Needless to say, no action was taken on the message.

It may be said, and perhaps rightly, that the situation with respect to districting, while detracting from the equality of popular representation in the House, has little bearing on the role of Congress in preserving federalist values. I am not so sure. It is significant, for one thing, that it is the states that draw the districts; one can hardly think the district lines would be the same had they been drawn from the beginning by Congress. Beyond this, however, the general motive and tendency of district deviations has quite clearly been to reduce urban power, not in the meaning of the census classification[32] but in the sense of the substantial cities. The tendency is so appreciable that not long ago a small town magazine assured its readers that while cities or towns of under 10,000 coupled with the farms accounted for only fifty-one per cent of the entire population, residents of such areas were numerically dominant in 265 of the 435 congressional districts, accounting for the choice of sixty-one per cent of the House (including eighteen of the twenty-one committee chairmen) in addition to their numerical dominance in the choice of seventy-five per cent of the Senate.[33] Traditionally, at least, a more active localism and resistance to new federal intrusion centers in this fifty-one per cent of Americans than in the other forty-nine

[32] The 1950 census classifies the "urban" as opposed to "rural" population on a basis that includes as "urban" all persons living in places of 2500 or more inhabitants, whether incorporated as cities, towns, boroughs or villages, or unincorporated places outside any urban fringe. See 1 BUREAU OF CENSUS, CENSUS OF POPULATION: 1950 xv-xvii (1952).

[33] Pathfinder, The Town Journal, June, 1953, pp. 26–27.

per cent. I should suppose that this is likely to continue; and that the figures, therefore, have some relevancy to an understanding of why presidential programs calling for the extension of national activity, and seemingly supported by the country in a presidential election, may come a cropper notwithstanding in the House. Such hostility to Washington may rest far less on pure devotion to the principle of local government than on oppositon to specific measures which Washington proposes to put forth. This explanation does not make the sentiment the less centrifugal in its effects. Federalism would have few adherents were it not, like other elements of government, a means and not an end.[34]

V

If Congress, from its composition and the mode of its selection, tends to reflect the "local spirit" predicted by Madison, the prime organ of a compensating "national spirit" is, of course, the President — both as the Chief Executive and as the leader of his party. Without the unifying power of the highest office, derived from the fixed tenure gained by the President's election and the sense that he speaks for and represents the full national constituency, it would be difficult to develop the centripetal momentum so essential to the total federal scheme. No modern President can doubt that one of his essential functions is to balance the localism and the separatism of the Congress by presenting programs that reflect the needs of the entire nation, building the best coalitions that he can for their enactment,[35] using the prerogatives and prestige

[34] For an interesting comment on this aspect of the matter in relation to Australian federalism see Partridge, *The Politics of Federalism* in FEDERALISM: AN AUSTRALIAN JUBILEE STUDY 174 (Sawer ed. 1952).

[35] On the weak hold of party ties on voting in the Congress, and especially the Senate, see, *e.g.*, HOLCOMBE, *op. cit. supra* note 10, at 152, 215.

of his office to that end.[36] That this has been accomplished, on the whole, despite the role allotted to the states in the selection of the President yields more support than Bagehot realized for his great dictum that "the men of Massachusetts could . . . work *any* Constitution."[37]

Fashioning the method to be followed in the choice of Presidents was, perhaps, the problem that the framers found it hardest to resolve.[38] To look for his selection to the Congress posed the danger of a servile Chief Executive, dependent for his reelection on the legislature he was meant to balance in the total scheme. Election by the people faced the powerful opponents of the franchise and the fear of turmoil if the country as a whole should be involved in any single choice. Any method raised the most divisive issue of the undertaking: the claims of large states to a recognition of their stature and the fears of small that if they lost equality they would lose all effective voice.

Macaulay's school boy knows the terms of the resulting compromise. The choice was vested neither in the Congress nor the people but in electors who would be appointed in each state for this one purpose in the manner that its legislature might provide. The number of electors showed a deference to population coupled with a reservation, the total resting not alone upon the number of the Representatives allotted

36 *Cf.* HYMAN, THE AMERICAN PRESIDENT 52–53 (1954): "His problem would be simplified if the coalition he built for an election-day victory remained stable. But it does nothing of the sort. . . . To get any kind of measure enacted, the President has to build a special coalition for the immediate object in view." See also, *e.g.*, WILSON, CONSTITUTIONAL GOVERNMENT IN THE UNITED STATES, c. III (1908); HERRING, PRESIDENTIAL LEADERSHIP (1940); Rowe, *Cooperation or Conflict? — The President's Relationships with an Opposition Congress*, 36 GEO. L.J. 1 (1947).

37 BAGEHOT, THE ENGLISH CONSTITUTION 296 (1914 ed.).

38 See, *e.g.*, 2 FARRAND, THE RECORDS OF THE FEDERAL CONVENTION (1937) 118 (Mason); 501 (Wilson); 3 *id.* 132, 331 (Madison); 166 (Wilson).

to a state in Congress but also on the Senators that did not vary with its size. To assure that the electors would be independent of the federal establishment, all national officials, including members of the Congress, were disqualified to serve. To prevent merely parochial determinations, each elector was to designate two persons, only one of whom could be of his own state. To eliminate all chance of intrigue — and perhaps to save expense as well — the electors were not to assemble in convention; meeting separately in their respective states on some one day fixed by the Congress, they were to cast their votes in insularity and be discharged. Finally, in further safeguard of the smaller states, a majority of all the votes — in addition to the largest number — was required for election of a President.[39] If no one person gained such widespread preference, the votes of the electors could do nothing more than effect nominations; the choice among the five with most electoral votes was transferred to the House of Representatives. In the House, substituted for the Senate at the final moment to avoid executive dependence on the smaller body, size was rendered wholly immaterial. The states were granted one vote each, regardless of the number of their Representatives, a majority of all the states required for election. After the choice of President, the candidate with most electoral votes was to be Vice President, the Senate authorized to break a tie.[40]

[39] It should be noted that the requirement of a majority meant far less with each elector casting two votes for President than it did after the adoption of the twelfth amendment. *Cf.* 2 FARRAND, *supra* note 38 at 512 (Morris).

[40] Only the time when the electors shall be chosen and the day when they shall vote are explicitly subjected to control by Congress. But since the electoral votes are counted in joint session of both Houses, it became accepted that theirs is the agency to settle issues that arise upon the counting. The aftermath of the Hayes-Tilden controversy was the Act of

If this complex solution yielded universal satisfaction at the time of ratification,[41] it was a sentiment that surely was short-lived. Whatever abstract merit was possessed by the idea of independent electors, the rise of parties swiftly made the concept obsolete. With party tickets in the field, the choice of two became impossible, yielding either a bipartisan result as in the third election or the tie between the victors[42] that produced the crisis of the fourth. The growth of the congressional caucus as a nominating agency made mockery of the intention to protect the choice from legislative domination. Freedom for state legislatures to provide the manner of appointment of electors led to great diversity in practice, the choice of method governed less by principle than by manipulation of controlling party factions and the wish to give the state as such the largest influence on the result.[43] If, as Madison averred,[44] the framers mainly contemplated that electors would be chosen in each state by districts through the action of those qualified to vote for Representatives, experience made

---

February 3, 1887, 24 STAT. 373, 3 U.S.C. § 6 (1946), designed to refer disputes as to the validity of state electoral votes to the state's courts, so far as possible.

41 *Cf.* HAMILTON, THE FEDERALIST No. 58: "The mode of appointment of the Chief Magistrate of the United States is almost the only part of the system, of any consequence, which has escaped without severe censure, or which has received the slightest mark of approbation from its opponents."

42 Hamilton concerned himself before the first election to prevent the unanimity in favor of George Washington from being matched by equal unanimity for Adams. See STANWOOD, A HISTORY OF THE PRESIDENCY 26 (1928).

43 Legislative choice, election by districts, and election by general ticket, or some combination thereof, are the principal methods involved. The diversities are summarized by Chief Justice Fuller in McPherson v. Blacker, 146 U.S. 1, 29–35 (1892). See also DOUGHERTY, THE ELECTORAL SYSTEM OF THE UNITED STATES 281–303 (1906). The methods used in each election are described in STANWOOD, *op. cit. passim.*

44 Letter to George Hay, August 23, 1823, quoted in 3 FARRAND, *supra* note 38 at 458–59.

clear that no state would long risk a division in the votes of its electors unless the method that made such division likely was decreed for all.[45]

Despite the magnitude of these initial difficulties, the twelfth amendment worked the only changes in the written Constitution and they were only marginal in their effects. It met the double-choice dilemma by providing for the separate designation of the presidential and vice-presidential choices; it reduced the range of choice committed to the House from five to three,[46] and it required a majority for choice of a Vice President by the electors, with the Senate otherwise empowered to select from only two.

Practice served, however, to resolve or soften other problems without changes in the document. The caucus was supplanted by the national convention, drawing broader popular participation to the nominating process.[47] The danger that electors might express the independent choice the law allowed them was diminished by the choice of party men to seek the office and the sentiment that no betrayal of the pledge would be condoned.[48] There was a steady drift within the states in the direction of the popular selection of electors, though the

45 *Cf.* Letter from Jefferson to Monroe, January 20, 1800, quoted in DOUGHERTY, *op. cit.* at 286: "All agree that an election by districts would be best if it could be general, but while ten States choose either by their Legislatures or by a general ticket, it is folly or worse than folly for the other six not to do it."

46 Since the twentieth amendment this has meant the new rather than the expiring House of Representatives but the matter is within control of Congress in virtue of its authority to determine the time when the electors are chosen and the day when they shall vote (article II, section 1), as well as when their votes shall be counted.

47 *Cf.* STANWOOD, *op. cit.* at 125.

48 STANWOOD (*op. cit.* at 5) quotes the following comment on the Pennsylvania Federalist elector who voted for Jefferson in 1796: "Do I chuse Samuel Miles to determine for me whether John Adams or Thomas Jefferson shall be President? No! I chuse him to act, not to think." On Plumer's

method that won dominance was the general ticket that cast the state's votes as a unit by selecting men of common sentiment rather than the district system under which its votes would normally divide.[49] Control of nominations in the early years by caucus and thereafter by convention, coupled with the instinct to support no more than two important parties, narrowed the range of choice sufficiently to yield electoral majorities. Such majorities have even been obtained despite third-party candidates, as in 1860, 1912, and 1948, thanks largely to the use of the general ticket in electing the electors; minority opinion has been sufficiently washed out within the states, without the fragmentation of their electoral votes. Only one election after 1800 — that of Adams over Jackson, ended in the House of Representatives[50] — where some, at least, of those who framed the system must have thought and hoped the choice would normally be made under the rule of state equality. It is not comfortable to reflect how far such a result might have reduced the President to a mere agent of

vote for John Quincy Adams in 1820, see Horwill, The Usages of the American Constitution 46–7 (1925).

James Russell Lowell answered the plea that he resolve the controversy of 1876 by giving Tilden the one vote he needed for election, as follows: "I was nominated and elected by my fellow-citizens of the Republican party to give effect to their political wishes as expressed at the polls, and not to express my own personal views . . . to refuse to comply with the mandate I received when I accepted my party's nomination would be treacherous, dishonorable, and immoral."

[49] South Carolina adhered to legislative selection until 1860 and this method was employed by Florida in 1868 and Colorado in 1876. Michigan adopted choice by districts briefly in 1892, the action challenged and sustained in McPherson v. Blacker, *supra* note 43. With these exceptions choice by general ticket appears to have been general after 1832.

[50] The division of electoral votes was Jackson: 99; Adams: 84; Crawford: 41; Clay: 37. The fact that Jackson led in tabulations of the popular vote was of small consequence since in six states the electors were chosen by the legislature and elsewhere the vote was very small. See Stanwood, *op. cit.* at 135, 140.

the states, exacerbating the intrinsic localism of the Congress, losing the unifying thrust for which the Presidency stands.

Fortunate though the result has been in keeping presidential choices from devolving on the House, the system still presents important difficulties. The fact that electoral votes are allocated to the states upon the basis of their population rather than the number of their voters means that the votes of individuals vary in influence depending on the size of the electorate within the states where they are cast.[51] Whatever merit there may be in the egalitarian objection, the state allocation must be taken as a datum of our federalism that is probably beyond the reach of an amendment. The other problems are, in any case, more serious. The system cannot meet third-party threats with any confidence if the third party has sufficient sectional strength to win state pluralities and thus to make a substantial showing in the electoral vote. If this contingency befalls, there is, as was made clear in 1948,[52] great danger of the choice devolving on the House. A third party also can exploit the use of the electors by running candidates who are unpledged or who affirm intent to act with independence on stated contingencies. Their selection in some states while others hold to the tradition would produce in any undecided contest an anomalous selecting body, composed partially of mere automata and partially of men free to appraise, negotiate, and choose. Moreover, disregard of the minorities within each

51 Thus in the 1948 election the ratio of electoral to popular votes ranged between 1 to 161,000 in California and 1 to 18,000 in South Carolina.

52 With thirty-nine electoral votes for Thurmond in 1948, small shifts of votes in Ohio and California, which Truman carried by 7107 and 17,865 respectively, would have sent the election to the House — where incidentally, only twenty-one state delegations were controlled by nondissenting Democrats, twenty were Republican controlled, and three were evenly divided. The four Thurmond states could thus have blocked any selection in the House or forced it on their terms.

state and of the size of the plurality by which a state is carried contracts the basis of our presidential politics, reducing the incentive to campaign in territory certain to return pluralities in favor of the opposition and focusing prime attention on the large and doubtful states. In addition, since small margins of difference may determine large and possibly decisive groups of electoral votes, voting blocs that may appear to hold the balance of decision in pivotal states are granted disproportionate political importance. Finally, there is the risk that a candidate may be defeated on electoral votes, even though he has a solid popular plurality. Thus Hayes prevailed in the disputed election despite Tilden's plurality of over 250,000 — even on Republican claims. Cleveland's lead of almost 100,000 did not prevent the choice of Harrison in 1888. Wilson needed his advantage of 3806 in California in the 1916 election though a reversal there would have left his national plurality at almost 600,000. The shift of only 29,000 votes in California, Illinois and Ohio would have elected Dewey in 1948, though Truman prevailed by 2,000,000 in the country.

It is much easier to state these difficulties than to find solutions to them, though more proposals of amendment have been offered on this subject than on any other aspect of the Constitution.[53] For roughly half of our history the most significant proposal was to require choice of electors by districts or, dispensing with electors, district determination of electoral votes. Such a plan, favored by Hamilton, Jefferson, and Madison, barely missed submission to the states in 1820; on four occa-

[53] A thorough summary to 1889 is provided in AMES, THE PROPOSED AMENDMENTS TO THE CONSTITUTION OF THE UNITED STATES DURING THE FIRST CENTURY OF ITS HISTORY (published as Volume II of the Annual Report of the American Historical Association and printed as H.R. Doc. No. 353, 54th Cong., 2d Sess.) at 75 *et seq.* See also DOUGHERTY, *op. cit.* at 325 *et seq.*

sions before 1824 it won the necessary two-thirds in the Senate only to fail of House consideration or support.[54] Benton was perhaps its strongest advocate before the Civil War,[55] Morton thereafter,[56] though the company was large indeed. Proportional division won support after Hayes-Tilden[57] and has since been the leading proposition,[58] its advocates joining the partisans of district choice in their attack upon the general ticket but adding in defense of their alternative that it more perfectly reflects the popular division and avoids the danger of a gerrymander which the use of districts would present.[59] Madison's original conception[60] of a direct, popular election

54 See AMES, *op. cit.* at 80, 113.

55 See, *e.g.*, SEN. REP. No. 22, 19th Cong., 1st Sess. (1826).

56 See, *e.g.*, SEN. REP. No. 395, 43d Cong., 1st Sess. (1874).

57 See AMES, *op. cit.* at 95–98; H.R. REP. No. 819, 45th Cong., 2d Sess. (1878). Had the plan been in effect it would have avoided the dispute, securing Tilden's election by 189.674 electoral votes to 175.925 for Hayes. See H.R. REP. No. 819, at p. 12 for the distribution.

58 The plan, sponsored by Congressman Lea, won unanimous approval of a House Committee in 1933 (H.R. REP. No. 2194, 72d Cong., 2d Sess.; H.R. REP. No. 262, 73d Cong., 1st Sess.). It failed to win support, however, in the Senate Judiciary Committee which favored retention of the unit rule but relaxation of the requirement of a majority to thirty-five per cent of the electoral votes (SEN. REP. No. 313, 73d Cong., 2d Sess.). More recently, both Judiciary Committees have supported a proportional division resolution. See, *e.g.*, SEN. REP. No. 1230, 80th Cong., 2d Sess. (1948); SEN. REP. No. 602, 81st Cong., 1st Sess. (1949); SEN. REP. No. 594, 82d Cong., 1st Sess. (1951); H.R. REP. No. 1615, 80th Cong., 2d Sess. (1948); H.R. REP. No. 1011, 81st Cong., 1st Sess. (1949); H.R. REP. No. 1858, 81st Cong., 2d Sess. (1950); H.R. REP. No. 1199, 82d Cong., 1st Sess. (1951). Such a proposal passed the Senate by the requisite two-thirds (64–27) in early 1950 but failed to win even a majority in the House (134–210). See 96 CONG. REC. 1278, 10427 (1950). Senator Ferguson and Representative Case both filed dissenting reports in 1949. See SEN. REP. No. 602, Part 2; H.R. REP. No. 1011 at 27. For the modification proposed by Mr. Case, see 96 CONG. REC. A 890, 891 (1950).

59 For Harrison's defense of the general ticket and his proposal that it be prescribed by amendment to prevent such action as Michigan's adoption of districts in 1892, see 9 RICHARDSON, MESSAGES AND PAPERS OF THE PRESIDENTS, 208.

60 2 FARRAND, *op. cit.*, 111.

— without the insulation of state units — has also had proponents but the plan has never had significant Congressional support.[61]

The provisions for election by the House have been no less a target than the general ticket, the attack launched with greatest fervor as the problem of the 1824 election was anticipated and as Jacksonians reflected on the choice.[62] There has, however, been much difference in suggested treatment of the failure of electoral majority. Benton, moved by Jackson's opposition to congressional participation upon any basis,[63] urged a second popular election for a choice between the two prevailing candidates.[64] Others offered the retention of selection by the Congress, abolishing the vote by states in favor of a vote per capita by Representatives alone or by the members of both Houses in joint session.[65] Some, finally, have held the view that a plurality of electoral votes should be enough.

This is too bare a summary to picture the incredible variety of the proposals offered but it suffices to depict the leading remedies submitted in the long debate.

Whatever may be said in principle for simple popular election, the change would so diminish the political importance of the states of small electorates that there plainly is no hope of its adoption. Any method calling for or likely to result in the division of a state's electoral votes is unacceptable upon the merits, so long as the House chooses on a vote by states on failure of electoral majority; the danger that elections may devolve upon the House would be increased. The real question, accordingly, is whether a division plan is workable upon a

[61] See AMES, *op. cit.* at 87. A proposal to empower Congress to "prescribe the manner in which the electors shall be chosen by the people" passed the Senate as a portion of the fifteenth amendment but failed to satisfy the House. *Id.* at 105.

[62] *Id.* at 106.

[63] See, *e.g.*, 2 RICHARDSON, *op. cit.*, 447.

[64] See note 55, *supra.*

[65] AMES, *op. cit.* at 107.

basis that either permits election by plurality, whatever its dimensions, or vests the election in the Congress as a whole, voting *per capita*, unless one candidate obtains a specified percentage of the electoral votes, such as the forty per cent required in the resolution approved in 1950 by the Senate.

There is something to be said for the proportional division plan, even beyond the point that it would be a gain for the Republic to eliminate the present possibility of House selection on a plane of state equality. Division would deny to voting blocs within a state any disproportionate strategic importance. Moreover, absent intense sectional concentration of voting allegiance, proportional division should provide a better mirror of popular opinion than the present system. But intense sectional concentration of allegiance does exist and it exists, moreover, in the states where the voting population represents the smallest fraction of the total population that determines the number of electoral votes. The division plan would greatly increase the relative influence of these states and reduce that of the states with large electorates, accustomed to a close division in their voting. In the election of 1900, for example, where McKinley had a popular plurality of 861,459, the division system would have elected Bryan because of the relative unity of his southern vote.[66]

To make the point in more detail, I cite the 1944 election, but the evidence that it affords is typical of most. The twelve southern states polling a total vote of 5,609,320 gave Roosevelt a plurality of 2,263,270, which brought him 138 electoral votes and yielded none to his opponent. Division would have cut his lead to 65+, giving him 99+ and Dewey 33+, with

[66] See the testimony of Basil Brewer, publisher of the New Bedford Standard-Times, *Hearings before Subcommittee of Senate Committee on the Judiciary on S. J. Res. 2*, 81st Cong., 1st Sess. 141–42 (1949).

4+ for minor candidates. California, Illinois, Michigan, New York and Pennsylvania — the five states with the largest voting population — all have active party competition. They cast a total vote of 20,621,569, returning a Roosevelt plurality of 1,026,256, giving him 135 electoral votes to 25 for Dewey, an advantage of 110. But proportional division would have brought this lead to less than 10, producing 83+ for Roosevelt to 73+ for Dewey. Thus a plurality within the single party states would have had an average worth of three times that given to a similar plurality in the states with the largest voting populations and the keenest party competition.

The point is made with greater emphasis by pointing to the situation in 1944 within individual states. California with 3,520,549 votes yielded Roosevelt a plurality of 475,599. Proportional division would have meant that this advantage was worth less than four electoral votes. New York gave Roosevelt a lead of 316,591 on a total vote of 6,316,790. Under division the electoral advantage would have been but slightly more than two. Yet South Carolina with 103,375 votes and a plurality for Roosevelt of 86,054 would have produced an electoral lead of almost seven votes. So Mississippi would have counted over seven in return for a plurality of 155,773 among 180,080; and Texas, showing an advantage of 630,180 out of 1,150,330 would have contributed a lead of almost thirteen votes.

The impact of the change is illustrated by considering its probable effect on party practice. Where the conventions now place emphasis upon the large and doubtful states, proportional division would inevitably turn it to the South — the Democrats to seek to hold their large advantage, the Republicans to reduce what would otherwise be a destructive lead. If the present emphasis on the pivotal states presents the evils that

I have already noted, it has at least the virtue of its limitations: on the whole, it centers party thought upon the needs and claims of the most numerous among us, compensating for the diminution of the influence that the electoral system gives their individual votes and balancing somewhat their underrepresentation in Congress. To shift this emphasis to the states which now combine the smallest of electorates with an exceptional influence in the Congress would present comparable evils, in directing political appeals to a limited area, without the mitigation of comparable gain.

The answer given is that the proportional division would provide its own corrective of this danger by creating party competition where it now is lacking; that this in turn would create pressures for enlarging the electorate and thus would bring two-party politics to the affected states. If this prediction is correct it is a potent answer — but the trouble is that it may turn out to be wrong. The change might work *per contra* to solidify adherence to one party and intensify desire for restriction of the franchise in order to retain the larger influence that solidarity would yield. The other states would then have no defense but imitation, as the states that first chose their electors on a district basis felt impelled by those that would not risk division to adopt the method that made unity the rule. But such an increase in the single party states would hardly leave us with the sense that we had made any advance. The people of the states of large electorates, confronted with this further diminution in the influence accorded to their members, may well prefer not to reflect their own internal difference of opinion, lest they imperil values larger than those involved in their differences, including their capacity to disagree.

What I have said about proportional division applies on

the whole to the proposal to require choice within the states by one-vote districts rather than by the states at large.[67] Though it would be more difficult to show the consequences in detail, this method also would enhance the influence of single-party states at the expense of those that show a close division, with the consequences that I have described.[68]

In net result, the present practice with respect to electoral votes seems likely to endure; and since both the use of the electors as the agency of choice and the House vote by states on failure of an electoral majority are probably unchangeable alone, these features of the system will probably remain as well, despite the weight and historicity of the objections to them.

Federalist considerations thus play an important part even in the selection of the President, although a lesser part than many of the framers must have contemplated. A presidential candidacy must be pointed towards the states of largest population in so far as they are doubtful. It must balance this direction by attention to the other elements of the full coalition that is looked to for an electoral majority. Both major parties have a strong incentive to absorb protest movements of such sectional significance that their development in strength would throw elections to the House. Both must give some attention to the organized minorities that may approach balance-of-power status in important states, without, however, making promises that will outrun the tolerance of other necessary elements of their required strength. Both parties recognize that they must appeal to some total combination of allegiance, choice, or in-

[67] For a contrary view, see, *e.g.*, Wilmerding, *Reform of the Electoral System*, 64 POL. SCI. Q. 1 (1949).

[68] See the study by Professor Ruth C. Silva (App. A-J) in *Hearings before a Subcommittee of the Senate Committee on the Judiciary on S. J. Res. 8, 17, 19, 55, 84, 85, 95, 100*, 83d Cong., 1st Sess. 230, 237–46 (1953).

terest that will yield sufficient nation-wide support to win elections and make possible effective government.

The most important element of party competition in this framework is the similarity of the appeal that each must make. This is a constant affront to those who seek purity of ideology in politics; it is the clue, however, to the success of our politics in the elimination of extremists — and to the tolerance and basic unity that is essential if our system is to work.[69]

The President must be, as I have said above, the main repository of "national spirit" in the central government. But both the mode of his selection and the future of his party require that he also be responsive to local values that have large support within the states. And since his programs must, in any case, achieve support in Congress — in so far as they involve new action — he must surmount the greater local sensitivity of Congress before anything is done.

VI

If this analysis is correct, the national political process in the United States — and especially the role of the states in the composition and selection of the central government — is intrinsically well adapted to retarding or restraining new intrusions by the center on the domain of the states. Far from a national authority that is expansionist by nature, the inherent tendency in our system is precisely the reverse, necessitating the widest support before intrusive measures of importance can receive significant consideration, reacting readily to opposition grounded in resistance within the states. Nor is this tendency effectively denied by pointing to the size or scope of the existing national establishment. However useful it may

[69] See Fischer, *op. cit. supra* note 14.

be to explore possible contractions in specific areas, such evidence points mainly to the magnitude of unavoidable responsibility under the circumstances of our time.

It is in light of this inherent tendency, reflected most importantly in Congress, that the governmental power distribution clauses of the Constitution gain their largest meaning as an instrument for the protection of the states. Those clauses, as is well known, have served far more to qualify or stop intrusive legislative measures in the Congress than to invalidate enacted legislation in the Supreme Court.

This does not differ from the expectation of the framers quite as markedly as might be thought. For the containment of the national authority Madison did not emphasize the function of the Court; he pointed to the composition of the Congress and to the political processes. So in his letter to Everett, written in 1830, he summarized the views that he had often stated:

> as a security of the rights and powers of the states in their individual capacities ag[ainst] an undue preponderance of the powers granted to the Government over them in their united capacity, the Constitution has relied on 1. The responsibility of the Senators and Representatives in the Legislature of the U.S. to the Legislatures & peoples of the States. 2. The responsibility of the President to the people of the U. States; & 3. The liability of the Ex. and Judiciary functionaries of the U.S. to impeachment by the Representatives of the people of the States, in one branch of the legislature of the U.S. and trial by the Representatives of the States, in the other branch; the State functionaries, Legislative, Executive & judiciary, being at the same time in their appointment & responsibility, altogether independent of the agency or authority of the U. States.[70]

[70] 9 Writings of James Madison 383, 395–96 (Hunt ed. 1910).

The prime function envisaged for judicial review — in relation to federalism — was the maintenance of national supremacy against nullification or usurpation by the individual states, the national government having no part in their composition or their councils.[71] This is made clear by the fact that reliance on the courts was substituted, apparently on Jefferson's suggestion,[72] for the earlier proposal to give Congress a veto of state enactments deemed to trespass on the national domain. And except for the brief interlude that ended with the crisis of the thirties, it is mainly in the realm of such policing of the states that the Supreme Court has in fact participated in determining the balances of federalism.[73] This is not to say that the Court can decline to measure national enactments by the Constitution when it is called upon to face the question in the course of ordinary litigation; the supremacy clause governs there as well. It is rather to say that the Court is on weakest ground when it opposes its interpretation of the Constitution to that of Congress in the interest of the states, whose repre-

[71] See, *e.g.*, THE FEDERALIST, No. 44 at 283 (Lodge ed. 1888); *id.*, No. 45 at 288; Madison: Letter to Everett, *supra* note 70; Letter to Thomas Ritchie, Dec. 18, 1825, *op. cit. supra* note 70 at 231; Letter to Jefferson, June 27, 1823, *id.* at 137, 140–44; Letter to Spencer Roane, June 29, 1821, *id.* at 65; Freund, *Umpiring the Federal System*, 54 COLUM. L. REV. 561, at 567 (1954).

[72] See his letter to Madison, June 20, 1787, quoted in WARREN, THE MAKING OF THE CONSTITUTION 168–69 (1928).

[73] Of the great controversies with respect to national power before the Civil War, only the Bank and slavery within the territories were carried to the Court and its participation with respect to slavery was probably its greatest failure. The question of internal improvements, for example, which raised the most acute problem of constitutional construction, was fought out politically and in Congress. After the War only the *Civil Rights Cases* and income tax decisions were important in setting limits on national power — until the *Child Labor Case* and the New Deal decisions. The recasting of constitutional positions since the crisis acknowledges much broader power in the Congress — as against the states — than it is likely soon or ever to employ.

sentatives control the legislative process and, by hypothesis, have broadly acquiesced in sanctioning the challenged Act of Congress.[74]

Federal intervention as against the states is thus primarily a matter for congressional determination in our system as it stands. So too, moreover, is the question whether state enactments shall be stricken down as an infringement on the national authority. For while the Court has an important function in this area, as I have noted, the crucial point is that its judgments here are subject to reversal by Congress, which can consent to action by the states that otherwise would be invalidated. The familiar illustrations in commerce and in state taxation of federal instrumentalities do not by any means exhaust the field.[75] The Court makes the decisive judgment only when — and to the extent that — Congress has not laid down the resolving rule.[76]

To perceive that it is Congress rather than the Court that on the whole is vested with the ultimate authority for managing our federalism is not, of course, to depreciate the role played by the Court, subordinate though it may be. It is no

[74] Surprisingly, Chief Justice Arthur Vanderbilt ignored this point in his lectures urging judicial control of congressional expenditures. See VANDERBILT, THE DOCTRINE OF THE SEPARATION OF POWERS AND ITS PRESENT-DAY SIGNIFICANCE 135–40 (1953).

[75] See *Mr. Justice Stone and the Constitution, infra* pp. 120, 125–126; Freund, *op. cit. supra* note 71, at 562.

[76] The judicial function in relation to federalism thus differs markedly from that performed in the application of those constitutional restraints on Congress or the states that are designed to safeguard individuals. In this latter area of the constitutional protection of the individual against the government, both federal and state, subordination of the Court to Congress would defeat the purpose of judicial mediation. For this is where the political processes cannot be relied upon to introduce their own correctives — except to the limited extent that individuals or small minorities may find a champion in some important faction. See Stone, J., in United States v. Carolene Products Co., 304 U.S. 144, 152–53 n. 4 (1938); *Mr. Justice Stone and the Constitution, infra* at pp. 129–130.

accident that Congress has been slow to exercise its managerial authority, remitting to the Court so much of what it could determine by a legislative rule. The difficulties of reaching agreement on such matters, not to speak of drafting problems of immense complexity, lend obvious attractiveness to the *ad hoc* judicial method of adjustment. Whether Congress could contribute more effectively to the solution of these problems is a challenging and open question. The legislative possibilities within this area of our polity have hardly been explored.

Mr. Justice Stone and the Constitution

ON April 22, 1946, an opinion day in the Supreme Court, Mr. Justice Douglas announced the decision in *Girouard v. United States.*[1] The question was whether unwillingness to bear arms because of pacifist religious belief is a bar to naturalization under the governing Act of Congress. In the cases of *Schwimmer*[2] and *Macintosh*[3] an earlier Court had held that under such circumstances naturalization must be denied, provoking the famous dissenting opinions of Justice Holmes and Chief Justice Hughes. Speaking for a majority of the present Court, Justice Douglas declared that the dissenters of former years were right; the *Schwimmer* and *Macintosh* decisions were overruled. Mr. Chief Justice Stone, who had joined in the dissent in the *Macintosh* case now expressed his dissent in this. In his view, Congress had since considered the specific issue posed by the Court's decisions and had indicated by reenactment of the statute its acquiescence in the interpretation they

NOTE: This paper appeared in an issue of the *Columbia Law Review* published shortly after the death of Chief Justice Stone and dedicated to his memory. See 46 COLUM. L. REV. 764 (1946).

1 328 U.S. 61 (1946).

2 United States v. Schwimmer, 279 U.S. 644 (1929).

3 United States v. Macintosh, 283 U.S. 605 (1931).

laid down. The problem being one of construction alone, it was the duty of the Court to abide by the congressional will. The Chief Justice had barely concluded his statement — so characteristic in its deference to the legislative branch of the government in what he conceived to be its appropriate sphere — when his speech faltered. Escorted from the bench by Justices Black and Reed, he lingered into the evening but not beyond. Death had summoned him at the height of his powers, intruding upon the very act of adjudication to pluck at the sleeve of his gown.

It was a few months longer than twenty-one years since Attorney General Stone had left the Department of Justice to take his place upon the Court. More than five thousand cases determined on the merits bore the mark of his judicial participation, not to speak of the thousands more in which petitions for review were denied. But decisions are a collective product, a monument more to the Court than to any of its members, so far does the conference room conceal their individual parts. The personal contribution of a justice inheres rather in his own opinions, projecting into the future, as they do, the stamp of his method and the exposition of his major ideas. The six hundred opinions of Justice Stone — whether for the Court or in dissent — coupled with his occasional pieces, are his legacy to the nation he so indefatigably served.

More than a third of the opinions deal with constitutional issues. It detracts from neither the scope nor the importance of opinions in other fields, to say that these constitute the major element of his judicial work.[4] For whatever the impor-

[4] For previous discussion of Justice Stone's constitutional opinions, see Dowling, Cheatham and Hale, *Mr. Justice Stone and The Constitution* 36 COLUM. L. REV. 351 (1936); Dowling, *The Methods of Mr. Justice Stone in Constitutional Cases* 41 COLUM. L. REV. 1160 (1941); KONEFSKY, CHIEF JUSTICE STONE AND THE SUPREME COURT (1945).

tance of the Supreme Court as the ultimate voice in the ordinary areas of judicial administration, its dominant role inheres in its special position in the American constitutional scheme. Within the range of contested litigation the Court sits not alone to expound the law that it is within the province of Congress to change but also, as Chief Justice Stone has put it, to "determine the boundaries and distribution of power under a federal constitutional system."[5]

I. The Court and the Constitution

The special function of the Court in the resolution of constitutional controversies has encountered attack from the beginning, but a century and a half of polemic inspired no uncertainty on the issue in the mind of Mr. Stone. "A study of the Federal Constitution and the conditions leading to its enactment" leaves "no reasonable doubt that the doctrine of Marbury against Madison is legally and historically sound."[6] The "history of the judicial function before the adoption of the Constitution, the language of the Constitution itself in Article VI and the long course of judicial decision, leave that question no longer debatable."[7] "To have formulated in written language a separation of governmental powers into state and national with specific limitations upon each, as the supreme law of the land, and to have denied to the courts the power to apply that law in the settlement of controversies pending before them, would have been not only contrary to the experience of the colonies but would have involved the performance of the functions of government in confusion and

5 Proceedings in Memory of Mr. Justice Sutherland, 323 U.S. xix (1944).

6 Stone, Law and Its Administration 135 (1915) (herinafter cited as "Hewitt Lectures").

7 Stone, *Fifty Years Work of the United States Supreme Court* 8 Ore. L. Rev. 248, 260 (1929), 53 A.B.A. Rep. 259 (1928).

in conflicts of authority which would have imperiled the success of the great experiment."[8] By vesting the power of judicial review "in the Supreme Court, a body removed from political activity and possessing no control over the armed forces or material resources of the nation, and by the method of its constitution removed from the immediate pressure of popular clamor, the Constitution insured the peace and order of the country and intrusted the civil liberty of its citizens to the body best adapted to preserve and perpetuate it."[9] Indeed, the "government of a continent of forty-eight states, each making and administering its own laws, together with a central government of limited powers, set over them for limited purposes, making and administering laws of its own within the same territory" has been made "practicable and tolerable" only because "its framework has admitted of the solution of the clashing demands of the interests it has created by judicial decision in conformity to the methods of the common law."[10]

Expressing these views as the occasion was presented from 1915 to 1936, Mr. Stone opposed before his judicial appointment all devices to limit or control judicial review, whether by recall, by sanctioning legislative reenactment, or by requiring more than a majority of the Court.[11] This was the burden of his participation as Attorney General in the presidential campaign of 1924; and even after his appointment to the Court he took pains to outline the technical difficulties that he perceived in the LaFollette proposal, while withholding comment on the "political issue."[12] The sum of his position

[8] HEWITT LECTURES 137–38. [9] *Id.* at 138.

[10] Stone, *The Common Law in the United States* 50 HARV. L. REV. 4, 22 (1936).

[11] See, *e.g.*, HEWITT LECTURES 155–58.

[12] Stone, *supra* note 7, at 261–64.

was that "in practice the device of the weighted statutes could only operate to effect a gradual transfer of constitutional powers from the executive and judicial branches of the government to the legislative," a "shifting of governmental powers as they have been distributed by the Constitution" not "as the result of judicial action based on the provisions of the great document itself" but "by increasing the power of one branch" of the government "at the expense of the other by resort to its own legislative action."

If judicial review thus enlisted Justice Stone's unqualified support as an "implement of government under a written constitution,"[13] no one recognized more keenly than he that it "brought to the judicial function a task of peculiar gravity and delicacy."[14] The difficulty of the task was mitigated, to be sure, by "the extraordinary prescience with which the instrument itself, by definition not embarrassingly meticulous, has succeeded . . . in distributing governmental power between national and state governments in substantial conformity to national and local interests."[15] We may add the point that many of the most important provisions of the Constitution — such, for example, as those prescribing the organization of the Congress and the major outlines of legislative procedure, can rarely be drawn in issue in the Court. But these are mitigations only; the major elements of the problem must be met by the way in which the judicial responsibility is discharged by the courts.

It was characteristic of Justice Stone that on this branch of the issue he turned first to the nature of "the instrument" and the spirit in which it was envisaged by the "great Chief Jus-

[13] Announcement of the death of Mr. Justice Brandeis, 314 U.S. viii (1941).

[14] Stone, *supra* note 10, at 21.

[15] *Id.* at 22.

tice."[16] In "setting up an enduring framework of government" the framers "undertook to carry out for the indefinite future and in all the affairs of men, those fundamental purposes which the instrument itself discloses." Hence the words of the Constitution are not to be read "as we read legislative codes which are subject to continuous revision with the changing course of events, but as the revelation of the great purposes which were intended to be achieved by the Constitution as a continuing instrument of government."[17] "In defining their scope something more is involved than consultation of the dictionary and the rules of English grammar. They are to be read as a vital part of an organic whole so that the high purpose which illumines every sentence and phrase of the instrument may be given effect in a consistent and harmonious framework of government."[18]

Some of the provisions of the Constitution, it is true, "are framed in terms of specific and more or less detailed command" offering "relatively narrow scope for treatment otherwise," but the "great constitutional guarantees and immunities of personal liberty and of property, which give rise to the most perplexing questions of constitutional law and government, are but statements of standards to be applied by courts according to the circumstances and conditions which call for their application."[19] In that area, certainly, the Constitution "is not an aggregate of hard and fast precepts to be handed on and followed from generation to generation. It is rather an indication of starting points for legal reasoning and of a technique for developing it, expressing the ideal of a reasonable

[16] For illustrations of his references to Marshall, see Stone, *supra* note 7, at 249; United States v. Butler, 297 U.S. 1, 84 (1936) (dissent).

[17] United States v. Classic, 313 U.S. 299, 316 (1941).

[18] Wright v. United States, 302 U.S. 583, 607 (1938).

[19] Stone, *supra* note 10, at 23.

exercise of the powers of politically organized society, than the subjection of government to inexorable commands imposed upon it in another age. In such a system there is need of continuity such as the not too rigid adherence to precedent may attain, but it is the continuity not of rules but of aims and ideals which will enable government in 'all the various crises of human affairs,' to continue to function and to perform its appointed task within the bounds of reasonableness."[20]

The "perpetual question of constitutional law" is thus "where the line is to be drawn which marks the boundary between the appropriate field of individual liberty and right and that of government action for the larger good, so as to insure the least sacrifice of both types of social advantage." This is "necessarily a question of degree which may vary with time and place."[21] What is constant is the spirit in which such issues are to be confronted and the method by which their solution is to be sought: "the process of appraisal of the experiences of the past and the present"[22] in the technique of the common law. The result is especially dependent upon the facts; the judge "must open his eyes to all those conditions and circumstances . . . in the light of which reasonableness is to be measured."[23] And in the ultimate resolution of the issues he will do well to consider whether it is his own standard of what is reasonable or "a considered judgment of what the community may regard as within the limits of the reasonable" that will "represent the sober second thought of the community," "the firm base on which all law must ultimately rest."[24] There are "two guiding principles of decision which ought never to be absent from judicial consciousness. One is that courts are concerned only with the power to enact statutes, not with

[20] *Id.* at 24. [21] *Id.* at 22, 23. [22] *Id.* at 23.
[23] *Id.* at 24. [24] *Id.* at 25.

their wisdom. The other is that, while unconstitutional exercise of power by the executive and legislative branches of the government is subject to judicial restraint, the only check upon our own exercise of power is our own sense of self-restraint. For the removal of unwise laws from the statute books appeal lies not to the courts but to the ballot and to the processes of democratic government."[25]

To this appraisal of the judicial function in constitutional cases, must be added a number of supplementary conceptions which are hardly of subordinate significance in the context of Justice Stone's thought.

"By a self-denying ordinance of immeasurable importance to the balanced functioning of the constitutional system, the courts, under the leadership of Marshall, have declared that every law duly passed is presumed to be constitutional, and that the burden is on him who assails it to establish its unconstitutionality beyond the reasonable doubts of objective-minded men."[26] That the presumption has many aspects is almost apparent on its face. In one dimension, perhaps the most important, it reaffirms the substantive point that in dealing with coordinate branches of the government constitutional prohibitions are not to be read narrowly by the courts. In another, it is a statement that the judicial issue in reviewing legislation is limited to whether the legislative judgment is grounded in a rational base. And since what is rational (though possibly unwise) turns so largely upon the facts, what is presumed may be said to be "the existence of facts supporting the legislative judgment,"[27] though the presumption may, in this respect, yield in the end to the facts. Whatever its precise

[25] United States v. Butler, 297 U.S. 1, 78–79 (1936) (dissent).

[26] Stone, *supra* note 10, at 25.

[27] Stone, J., in United States v. Carolene Products Co., 304 U.S. 144, 152 (1938).

limits,[28] it was for Justice Stone a "check upon any excess of judicial power"[29] as well as an assurance that the processes of adjudication will so far as possible be fully informed.[30]

No less important than the presumption of validity in the operation of judicial review is the limitation of constitutional adjudication to the confines of the genuinely contested case. What is involved is not only an assurance that the issues will be fully presented to the Court but the equally important assurance that the courts will intrude in the constitutional process only when the need for their participation is acute. To this insulating doctrine Justice Stone fully subscribed. He joined in the great opinion of Justice Brandeis that put its application to the acid test in the case of the Tennessee Valley Authority;[31] and in many opinions of his own he applied the principle[32] and traced its subordinate procedural corollaries, serving in the aggregate to discipline federal injunctions restraining the enforcement of state legislation on constitutional grounds.[33] His preference, we may be sure, was that issues involving the validity of state action find their way to the Su-

[28] See the famous *Carolene Products* footnote (304 U.S. at 152–53) and the discussion *infra* p. 129 *et seq.*

[29] Stone, *supra* note 10, at 25.

[30] Stone, *supra* note 7, at 259–60.

[31] Ashwander v. Tennessee Valley Authority, 297 U.S. 288, 341 (1936); see also, *e.g.*, Cardozo, J., in Helvering v. Davis, 301 U.S. 619, 639 (1937).

[32] See, *e.g.*, Alabama State Federation of Labor v. McAdory, 325 U.S. 450 (1945); Coffman v. Breeze Corporations, 323 U.S. 316 (1945); Pacific Telephone and Telegraph Co. v. Seattle, 291 U.S. 300 (1934); Frost v. Corp. Commission, 278 U.S. 515, 552 (1929) (dissent); Railroad Comm. v. Los Angeles R. Co., 280 U.S. 145, 166 (1929) (dissent).

[33] See, *e.g.*, American Federation of Labor v. Watson, 327 U.S. 582, 600 (1946) (dissent); Douglas v. City of Jeannette, 319 U.S. 157 (1943); Great Lakes Dredge and Dock Co. v. Huffman, 319 U.S. 293 (1943); Natural Gas Co. v. Slattery, 302 U.S. 300 (1937); Beal v. Missouri Pacific R.R., 312 U.S. 45 (1941); Matthews v. Rodgers, 284 U.S. 521 (1932); Stratton v. St. Louis Southwestern Ry., 284 U.S. 530 (1932); Edelman v. Boeing Air Transp., 289 U.S. 249 (1933); Healy v. Ratta, 292 U.S. 263 (1934).

preme Court after preliminary examination in the state courts. But in this, as in other matters, his interest was in substance and not in form. Insistence upon a proper standing to challenge legislation, upon the imminence of injury, the presence of adverse parties, and the necessity for the constitutional test was not to be made the occasion for obstructing procedural change that left these essentials untouched. "The judiciary clause of the Constitution defined and limited judicial power, not the particular method by which that power might be invoked."[34] In procedural matters no less than in substantive it is the duty of the Court, so far as the Constitution permits, to reconcile progress and tradition.[35] It is in these terms that he differed sharply with Justice Brandeis on the particular issue of the declaratory judgment; and he eventually carried the Court.[36]

To delineate Justice Stone's most general conceptions of the part of the Court in the constitutional process, I have drawn generally on his writings, deliberately disregarding differences of circumstance, time, or place. With respect to the issues thus far considered this is possible without distortion; to carry the method further would subordinate unduly what is to be per-

[34] Nashville C. & St. Louis Ry. v. Wallace, 288 U.S. 249, 264 (1933).

[35] See Gasoline Products Co. v. Champlin Refining Co., 283 U.S. 494 (1931), and the dissent in Dimick v. Schiedt, 293 U.S. 474, 490 (1935), where Justice Stone said with respect to the seventh amendment: "Such a provision of a great instrument of government, intended to endure for unnumbered generations, is concerned with substance and not with form. There is nothing in its history or language to suggest that the Amendment had any purpose but to preserve the essentials of the jury trial as it was known to the common law before the adoption of the Constitution. For that reason this Court has often refused to construe it as intended to perpetuate in changeless form the *minutiae* of trial practice as it existed in the English courts in 1791." *Cf.* District of Columbia v. Clawans, 300 U.S. 617 (1937).

[36] See Nashville C. & St. Louis Ry. v. Wallace, 288 U.S. 249 (1933); Willing v. Chicago Auditorium Ass'n, 277 U.S. 274, 290 (1928); Fidelity National Bank & Trust Co. v. Swope, 274 U.S. 123 (1927).

ceived of change and growth. No one can turn from the Hewitt lectures to Justice Stone's opinions or to his Harvard address without perceiving a shift in more than emphasis; there is, of course, discernible development in his opinions as they were written throughout the years. This is, indeed, to understate the point. The decades in question transformed the country; there was change hardly less than revolutionary in its dominant legal thought. If Justice Stone was a spectator of the social and economic development, his was very close to the major role in the authoritative definition of its impact upon the fundamental law. To measure his full contribution is more than the work of a single appreciation. I shall content myself with illustrating its scope in the most familiar fields.

II. The Power to Govern

When Justice Stone came to the Court, the dominant problem of American public affairs was that of marshaling the capacities of government to promote individual welfare by ordering the economic forces that industrial enterprise had unloosed. Efforts to surmount the problem had encountered, in addition to its inherent difficulties, conceptions antipathetic to government that had prevailed for a long time. Such conceptions might be defeated at the ballot box; it was more difficult to overcome them at the bar of the Supreme Court. Restrictive applications of the due process and equal protection clauses of the fourteenth amendment weighed heavily on the power of the states; and a narrow interpretation of the commerce clause especially in the child labor cases[37] stood athwart congressional action of fundamental economic reach.

[37] Hammer v. Dagenhart, 247 U.S. 251 (1918); see also Bailey v. Drexel Furniture Co., 259 U.S. 20 (1922).

However the issue might be posed in concrete cases, the portent was that governmental action must confine itself to narrow limits if the judicial test was to be survived.

Justice Stone's part in overturning this entrenched position is now a thrice-told tale. The lines had been drawn by Holmes and reinforced by Brandeis; Stone made clear in the first years of his service the side of the lines on which he stood.[38] A decade of persistent dissent made its progressive impact, as Holmes was replaced by Cardozo in 1932. By 1937, in the shadow of the Court plan, the dissenters had become a majority of the Court. When the changes in personnel had been effected, their protest had become the major premises of the Court. If Justice Stone was a junior in the pioneering effort, it fell to him to carry through the victory and then to consolidate the gain.

Despite the familiarity of the story, we shall do well to assemble the details.

The Taxing Power

Any expansion in the commitments of government presupposes wide latitude in exercising the power to tax. Moreover, since taxation combines detriment to the taxpayer with benefit to those who escape, the power is more than a device for the raising of revenue; it is an indispensable means of promoting social service and of directing the energies of enterprise along legislatively determined lines. We may exclude

38 See 2 PRINGLE, THE LIFE AND TIMES OF WILLIAM HOWARD TAFT 1044 (1939), for Mr. Taft's lament in 1929 that Stone "has ranged himself with Brandeis and with Holmes in a good many of our constitutional differences."

It has been noted that from the October Term 1925 until the end of the 1935 term, Justice Stone wrote 42 dissenting opinions and recorded additionally 98 dissenting votes, dissenting more frequently than any of his brethren in the second half of the decade. See Dowling, Cheatham and Hale, *supra* note 4, at 352, n. 4.

from present consideration cases which posed problems of jurisdiction or of commerce inherent in the federal system. Even when these issues were lacking, legislative judgment in selecting the subjects, the measure and the incidence of taxation met the challenge of arbitrariness and discrimination repeatedly urged before the Court. Whether the tax was state[39] or federal,[40] Justice Stone maintained in the broadest terms the freedom of legislative choice. When the Court divided, as it frequently did, he was almost invariably on the government side.[41] *Colgate v. Harvey*[42] at the 1935 term will serve to illustrate the issue and the nature of the position he espoused. Vermont levied a tax on income bearing securities but exempted interest on loans made within the state at not more

39 See Stebbins v. Riley, 268 U.S. 137 (1925); General American Tank Car Corp. v. Day, 270 U.S. 367 (1926); Roberts & Schaefer Co. v. Emmerson, 271 U.S. 50 (1926); Saltonstall v. Saltonstall, 276 U.S. 260 (1928); New York v. Latrobe, 279 U.S. 421 (1929); Carley & Hamilton v. Snook, 281 U.S. 66 (1930); Pacific Co., Ltd. v. Johnson, 285 U.S. 480 (1932); Lawrence v. State Tax Commission, 286 U.S. 276 (1932); Puget Power & Light Co. v. Seattle, 291 U.S. 619 (1934); Welch v. Henry, 305 U.S. 134 (1938); Clark v. Paul Gray, Inc., 306 U.S. 583 (1939); Charleston Federal Savings & Loan Ass'n v. Alderson, 324 U.S. 182 (1945); Fernandez v. Wiener, 66 Sup. Ct. 178 (1945). And see the dissenting opinions in Quaker City Cab Co. v. Pennsylvania, 277 U.S. 389, 412 (1928); Colgate v. Harvey, 296 U.S. 404, 436 (1935); Georgia Railway & Electric Co. v. Decatur, 295 U.S. 165, 171 (1935); Great Northern Ry. v. Weeks, 297 U.S. 135, 153 (1936).

40 See Bromley v. McCaughn, 280 U.S. 124 (1929); Milliken v. United States, 283 U.S. 15 (1931); Phillips v. Dime Trust and Safe Deposit Co., 284 U.S. 160 (1931); McLaughlin v. Alliance Insurance Co., 286 U.S. 244 (1932); Detroit Bank v. United States, 317 U.S. 329 (1943). And see the dissent in Heiner v. Donnan, 285 U.S. 312, 332 (1932).

41 In addition to his dissenting opinions *supra* notes 39 and 40, see his concurrence in the dissents of others, *e.g.*, Holmes, J., in Schlesinger v. Wisconsin, 270 U.S. 230, 241 (1926); Holmes, J., and Brandeis, J., in Untermyer v. Anderson, 276 U.S. 440, 446 (1928); Cardozo, J., in Liggett Co. v. Lee, 288 U.S. 517, 580 (1933); Anglo-Chilean Corp. v. Alabama, 288 U.S. 218, 229 (1933); Concordia Insurance Co. v. Illinois, 292 U.S. 535, 550 (1934); Stewart Dry Goods Co. v. Lewis, 294 U.S. 550, 566 (1935).

42 296 U.S. 404 (1935).

than five per cent. A majority held the discrimination untenable, both as a denial of equal protection and, by novel affirmation, an impairment of the privileges and immunities of citizens of the United States. A single sentence in Justice Stone's dissent made clear that the privileges and immunities doctrine was destined for short life: "Citizens of the United States are given no privilege not to pay taxes."[43] His reply on the equal protection point epitomizes the position he advanced whenever the occasion arose:

> All taxes must of necessity be levied by general rules capable of practical administration. In drawing the line between the taxed and the untaxed the equal protection clause does not command the impossible or the impractical. Unless the line which the state draws is so wide of the mark as palpably to have no reasonable relation to the legitimate end, it is not for the judicial power to reject it and say that another must be substituted.[44]

Colgate v. Harvey was overruled at the 1940 Term[45] but three years before, Justice Stone had written his views firmly into law in sustaining Alabama's Unemployment Compensation Act and the payroll tax by which the system was maintained.[46] The employer's challenge was addressed not only to the incidence of the tax but also to the purposes for which it was imposed. But neither attack served to erect a constitutional bar. "A legislature is not bound to tax every member of a class or none." "Where the public interest is served one business may be left untaxed and another taxed, in order to promote the one or to restrict or suppress the other." Whether

[43] *Id.* at 449. [44] *Id.* at 442.
[45] Madden v. Kentucky, 309 U.S. 83 (1940).
[46] Carmichael v. Southern Coal & Coke Co., 301 U.S. 495 (1937).

"the present expenditure serves a public purpose is a practical question addressed to the law-making department, and it would require a plain case of departure from every public purpose which could reasonably be conceived to justify the intervention of a court."[47] "The United States and the State of Alabama are not alien governments. They coexist within the same territory. Unemployment within it is their common concern. Together the two statutes now before us embody a cooperative legislative effort by state and national governments for carrying out a public purpose common to both which neither could fully achieve without the cooperation of the other. The Constitution does not prohibit such cooperation."[48]

This is not, of course, to deny that it is cause for concern that the tax structures of the nation and the states should so far as possible be coherent and just. It is to say that putting aside special considerations in the maintenance of the federal system, Justice Stone saw little in the Constitution, or, we may be sure, in the competence of the Supreme Court to prescribe how these ends should be attained.

The Police Power

Government regulation faced an even firmer hazard than taxation but the story by which it was surmounted runs a very similar course. The spirit of *Lochner v. New York*[49] had lost some of its grip on the Court by the time of Justice Stone's appointment[50] but its hold was firm in the face of

[47] *Id.* at 509, 512, 515. [48] *Id.* at 526.

[49] 198 U.S. 144 (1905).

[50] For Justice Stone's opinions for the Court sustaining state action in this area see Fort Smith Light and Traction Co. v. Paving District, 274 U.S. 387 (1927); Ohio *ex rel.* Clarke v. Deckebach, 274 U.S. 392 (1927); Miller v. Schoene, 276 U.S. 272 (1928); Standard Oil Co. v. Marysville, 279 U.S.

fundamental regulation[51] and especially the control of price or wage. Early in his judicial service Justice Stone came to grips with price. In *Tyson Bros. v. Banton*[52] and *Ribnik v. McBride*[53] the Court, in opinion by Justice Sutherland, found neither the resale of theatre tickets in New York nor the fees of private employment agencies in New Jersey "affected with a public interest." Price regulation fell in both cases before the ancient dictum of Lord Hale. Justice Stone's attack upon both formula and application makes us wonder today how the battle could ever have been fought. "I cannot accept as valid the distinction . . . that granted constitutional power to regulate there is any controlling difference between reasonable regulation of price, if appropriate to the evil to be remedied, and other forms of appropriate regulation which curtail liberty of contract or the use and enjoyment of property."[54] Lest logic should be insufficient to teach the lesson, it was buttressed in the *Ribnik* case by an exhaustive array of the facts about private employment agencies which made manifest the existence of the evil that the legislature had sought to meet. The heresy of 1928 became gospel in 1934, though minimum

582 (1929); Hardware Dealers Mutual Fire Insurance Co. v. Glidden Co., 284 U.S. 151 (1931); Metropolitan Co. v. Brownell, 294 U.S. 580 (1935); Asbury Hospital v. Cass County, 326 U.S. 207 (1945).

51 See, *e.g.*, Weaver v. Palmer Bros. Co., 270 U.S. 402 (1926); Frost v. Corporation Commission, 278 U.S. 515 (1929); New State Ice Co. v. Liebmann, 285 U.S. 262 (1932) in which Justice Stone joined in the dissent. For a rare instance in which Justice Stone was with the majority, Holmes and Brandeis dissenting, see Liggett Co. v. Baldridge, 278 U.S. 105 (1928) (Pennsylvania statute prohibiting corporate ownership of pharmacy or drugstore unless all stockholders are licensed pharmacists).

52 273 U.S. 418 (1927).

53 277 U.S. 350 (1928).

54 *Id.* at 373. But note that while Justice Holmes dissented, Justices Brandeis and Stone concurred in the result when the Court invalidated the Tennessee gasoline price control law in 1929. Williams v. Standard Oil Co., 278 U.S. 235 (1929).

rather than maximum prices were what the *Nebbia* case[55] involved.

With price regulation out of the shadow, the question of wage remained. The issue came to the Court from New York before the election of 1936, to be turned aside on highly technical grounds.[56] Not content with Chief Justice Hughes' dissenting effort to distinguish the earlier cases, Justice Stone met the issue head on:

> It is not for the courts to resolve doubts whether the remedy by wage regulation is as efficacious as many believe, or is better than some other, or is better even than the blind operation of uncontrolled economic forces. The legislature must be free to choose unless government is to be rendered impotent. The Fourteenth Amendment has no more embedded in the Constitution our preference for some particular set of economic beliefs than it has adopted, in the name of liberty, the system of theology which we may happen to approve.[57]

A year later the battle was over when the Washington law was sustained.[58] From that time forth there was no doubt that whatever lines might ultimately be drawn, the States had regained the power to govern, save as the power might be limited in reference to national needs.[59] But in the interim an even more important struggle had almost run its course, that of the nation to marshal its own power and resources for the solution of nation-wide problems.

[55] Nebbia v. New York, 291 U.S. 502 (1934). See also Borden's Co. v. Ten Eyck, 297 U.S. 251 (1936); O'Gorman & Young v. Hartford Insurance Co., 282 U.S. 251 (1931); Home Building & Loan Ass'n v. Blaisdell, 290 U.S. 398 (1934). Ribnik v. McBride, 277 U.S. 350 (1928), was explicitly overruled in Olsen v. Nebraska, 313 U.S. 236 (1941).

[56] Morehead v. New York *ex rel.* Tipaldo, 298 U.S. 587 (1936).

[57] *Id.* at 636.

[58] West Coast Hotel Co. v. Parrish, 300 U.S. 379 (1937).

[59] See pp. 112–126, *infra.*

The Constitutional Crisis

Prior to the explosive issues engendered by the Roosevelt program the capacity of the great vehicles of national power embodied in the Constitution had not, during Justice Stone's service, been the subject of acute consideration.[60] When the first test of the New Deal came in *Panama Refining Co. v. Ryan*,[61] the Petroleum Code fell on the ground of excessive delegation; only Justice Cardozo thought that on this point the legislation could survive. The *Gold Clause* cases came next, with a narrow escape for the government in the case of the government bond,[62] Justice Stone concurring, however, only in result.[63] The *Gold Clause* cases were followed promptly by the amazing judgment invalidating the Railroad Retirement Act,[64] Justices Stone, Brandeis and Cardozo join-

[60] See, however, the tax cases cited *supra* note 40 and Untermyer v. Anderson, 276 U.S. 440 (1928). And see also Justice Stone's opinions in Chicago, Rock Island & Pacific Ry. v. United States, 284 U.S. 80, 100 (1931) (dissent); Texas & Pacific Ry. v. United States, 289 U.S. 627, 655 (1933) (dissent); United States v. Illinois Central R. R., 291 U.S. 457, 464 (1934) (concurring); Illinois Commerce Comm. v. United States, 292 U.S. 474 (1934); Central Vermont Transportation Co. v. Durning, 294 U.S. 33 (1935).

[61] 293 U.S. 388 (1935). See generally, JACKSON, THE STRUGGLE FOR JUDICIAL SUPREMACY (1941).

[62] Perry v. United States, 294 U.S. 330 (1935).

[63] Finding the bondholder without remedy because of the government's immunity to suit for performance and the fact that no special damage had been proved in the Court of Claims, the Court nevertheless affirmed that there was constitutional infirmity in the nullification of the government obligation. Justice Stone thought that either the Court should rest on the immunity alone or else it should recognize that the immunity to suit demonstrated more than the absence of a remedy; that, as a matter of constitutional interpretation, when the power to regulate the value of money encountered an obligation deriving its force from the borrowing power, the former must be held to prevail. This view is reiterated in Justice Stone's concurrence in Smyth v. United States, 302 U.S. 329, 360 (1937). See also his dissent in Guaranty Trust v. Henwood, 307 U.S. 247, 264 (1939).

[64] Retirement Board v. Alton Railroad, 295 U.S. 330 (1935).

ing in the dissent of Chief Justice Hughes. Three weeks later the Recovery Act was stricken down,[65] the Court unanimous that the delegation was too wide. The opinion by Chief Justice Hughes found, however, in addition, that neither labor conditions nor marketing practices in the New York live poultry industry were within reach of the power of Congress under the commerce clause. Justice Stone joined Justice Cardozo in concurring on the delegation point as well as on the labor provisions, without addressing themselves to the market regulations, which they did not think a severable feature of the Code.[66]

Three major developments followed at the next term. The Tennessee Valley Authority was sustained with respect to Wilson Dam, though Justice Stone, as we have noted, was among those who thought, with Justice Brandeis, that the merits should not have been reached.[67] But the Agricultural Adjustment Act fell with a declaration that Congress could not use its spending power to induce farmers to reduce their crops — agriculture being exclusively an affair of the states.[68] The Bituminous Coal Conservation Act was brought down thereafter on the ground that the mining of coal constitutes "production" rather than "commerce" despite the dependence of the entire country on its use;[69] labor conditions in coal mining were also the exclusive affair of the states. Reading the decisions together the Social Security Act seemed doomed; and it was difficult to perceive how the National Labor Rela-

65 Schechter Corp. v. United States, 295 U.S. 495 (1935); see Stern, *The Commerce Clause and the National Economy* 59 HARV. L. REV. 645 (1946).

66 On the same day the court unanimously invalidated the Frazier-Lemke Farm Mortgage Act, though in terms that created no fundamental issue. Louisville Bank v. Radford, 295 U.S. 555 (1935).

67 Ashwander v. T.V.A., 297 U.S. 288 (1936).

68 United States v. Butler, 297 U.S. 1 (1936).

69 Carter v. Carter Coal Co., 298 U.S. 238 (1936).

tions Act could succeed under the standards by which the Coal Act had failed. Chief Justice Hughes and Justice Cardozo each filed dissents in the coal case, in which Justices Brandeis and Stone concurred; the dissent in *United States v. Butler* was written by Justice Stone, with the concurrence of Justices Brandeis and Cardozo alone.[70]

Justice Stone's dissent in the *Butler* case marks in many ways the high moment of the constitutional conflict. The technical issue seems so clear today that it is pedantic to describe it at length. Congress may tax and spend for the general welfare of the nation. So much the majority agreed. The actual plan left farmers free to reject the offered benefits and plant their crops, indeed to profit from the scarcity that might be created by others who agreed with the government to curtail their production. Justice Roberts, nevertheless, declared for the Court that Congress, assumed to lack power to command the farmer to reduce his crops, "may not indirectly accomplish those ends by taxing and spending to purchase compliance." Hence the processors, upon whom the tax was laid and who unquestionably might be subjected to a tax, were adjudged to be constitutionally exempt. The position encountered the ridicule of Justice Stone:

> The government may give seeds to farmers, but may not condition the gift upon their being planted in places where they are most needed or even planted at all. The government may give money to the unemployed, but may not ask that those who get it shall give labor in return, or even use it to support their families. It may give money to sufferers from earthquake, fire, tornado, pestilence or flood, but may not im-

[70] 297 U.S. 1, 78 (1936). See also Ashton v. Cameron County Dist., 298 U.S. 513 (1936), holding the Municipal Bankruptcy Act invalid as an invasion of the rights of the states, Hughes, C. J., Brandeis, J., and Stone, J., joining Cardozo, J., in dissent. *Id.* at 532.

> pose conditions — health precautions designed to prevent the spread of disease, or induce the movement of population to safer or more sanitary areas. All that, because it is purchased regulation infringing state powers, must be left for the states, who are unable or unwilling to supply the necessary relief.[71]

Even more significant, however, than Justice Stone's reply on the merits is his reminder that the only check upon the Court is "our own sense of self-restraint";[72] that "the conscience and patriotism of the Congress and the Executive" are also a restraint on the abuse of power; that "interpretation of our great charter of government" leads to destruction when it "proceeds on any assumption that the responsibility for the preservation of our institutions is the exclusive concern of any one of the three branches of government."[73] This was more than an answer to the specific issues. It was a general challenge to the majority of the Court. In the battle that followed it was the standard of the attack.

The story moves swiftly thereafter. On March 29, 1937, during the pendency of the Court plan, the Court sustained the collective bargaining provisions of the Railway Labor Act[74] — the same day the Washington minimum wage law and a revision of the Act for the relief of farm debtors[75] were upheld. The opinion in the *Railway* case was read by Justice Stone.[76] Two weeks later the Wagner Act survived the judicial test.[77] The judgments sustaining the Social Security

[71] 297 U.S. 1, 85 (1936). [72] *Id.* at 79.

[73] *Id.* at 87–88.

[74] Virginian Ry. v. Federation, 300 U.S. 515 (1937).

[75] West Coast Hotel Co. v. Parrish, 300 U.S. 379 (1937); Wright v. Vinton Bank, 300 U.S. 440 (1937).

[76] See also Sonzinsky v. United States, 300 U.S. 506 (1937).

[77] N.L.R.B. v. Jones & Laughlin, 301 U.S. 1 (1937), and companion cases.

Act followed, Justice Cardozo writing in support of the federal statute[78] and Justice Stone, as we have noted, in defense of the act of a State.[79] At the end of the term Justice Van Devanter retired to be replaced by Justice Black; and in rapid succession thereafter Justices Reed, Frankfurter, Douglas, and Murphy filled the places of Justices Cardozo, Sutherland, Brandeis, and Butler. A new court had come to judgment and its principal link between the past and the future was to be Mr. Justice Stone.

The Judicial Settlement

We have recalled Justice Stone's role in the constitutional crisis; we must examine his part as the terms of settlement were defined. In *National Labor Relations Board v. Fainblatt*[80] he made clear that the Wagner Act decisions were not to be read as a half measure; unfair labor practices were not beyond federal power because their effect upon interstate commerce was small. *Mulford v. Smith*[81] showed, in opinion by Justice Roberts, that by the exclusion of surplus farm products from an interstate market under the commerce power Congress could attain by compulsion what the *Butler* decision had held it could not buy. The decision invalidating the Railroad Retirement Act was swept aside in *United States v. Lowden*[82] with opinion by Justice Stone. And it was Justice Stone who, shortly before he became Chief Justice, wrote for the Court sustaining the Fair Labor Standards Act of 1938.[83]

78 Steward Machine Co. v. Davis, 301 U.S. 548 (1937); Helvering v. Davis, 301 U.S. 619 (1937).

79 Carmichael v. Southern Coal & Coke Co., 301 U.S. 495 (1937).

80 306 U.S. 601 (1939).

81 307 U.S. 38 (1939).

82 308 U.S. 225 (1939).

83 United States v. Darby Lumber Co., 312 U.S. 100 (1941); Opp Cotton Mills v. Administrator, 312 U.S. 126 (1941). See also Justice Stone's earlier

Hammer v. Dagenhart, the source of the dogma that the commerce power does not reach to manufacture was laid to rest at long last, with the comment that it constituted "a departure from the principles which have prevailed in the interpretation of the commerce clause both before and since the decision." A similar, though gentler disposition was made of *Carter v. Carter Coal Co.* which, indeed, had already fallen under the weight of the Wagner Act decision and the judgment sustaining the Bituminous Coal Act as amended in 1937.[84] In addition, Justice Stone explicitly rejected the contention, given force in the *Butler* and *Carter* decisions, that limitations upon the scope of the enumerated powers of Congress can be derived from the tenth amendment. "The Amendment states but a truism that all is retained which has not been surrendered."[85]

The *Darby* case involved both prohibition of interstate shipment of articles produced under the substandard conditions and the direct application of the standards to all employees engaged in production for commerce interstate. In sustaining the latter provisions Justice Stone took broad ground: "The power of Congress over interstate commerce is not confined to the regulation of commerce among the states. It extends to those activities intrastate which so affect interstate commerce or the exercise of the power of Congress over it as to make regulation of them appropriate means to the attainment of a legitimate end, the exercise of the granted power of Congress to regulate interstate commerce."[86] This, to be sure, was no new principle, as Justice Stone was at pains to

opinion in United States v. Carolene Products Co., 304 U.S. 144 (1938) (prohibiting shipment in interstate commerce of "filled milk").

[84] Sunshine Coal Co. v. Adkins, 310 U.S. 381 (1940).

[85] 312 U.S. 100, 124 (1941).

[86] 312 U.S. 100, 118 (1941).

point out. What was novel was the indication that henceforth it was to be given full scope. In *United States v. Wrightwood Dairy Co.*[87] at the 1941 term the principle was applied, in opinion by Justice Stone, to sustain federal regulation of the price of milk produced and sold intrastate in competition with similarly regulated milk moving into the market from outside the state.[88] *Wickard v. Filburn*,[89] in which Justice Stone joined, carried a further step. The fact that wheat grown for consumption on the farm satisfies a demand that would otherwise seek satisfaction in the market sufficed to extend a federal crop reduction order to production for the farm alone. Thus there was little doubt before the Chief Justice's last term that the commerce power confers upon Congress a regulatory authority in the economic realm that is as broad as it is ever likely to employ.[90]

Quite as important as the commerce question posed by the Fair Labor Standards Act was the charge that it embodied an unduly generous delegation of power. Attacks upon delegation had, indeed, lost their old magic as the Agricultural Adjustment Act of 1938, the Bituminous Coal Act of 1937, and the Agricultural Marketing Agreement Act were successively sustained. The complex task of imposing controls on the economy puts a unique demand that legislative standards shall be general with flexible administrative implementation. In this milieu especially no formula can substitute for practical judgment in determining whether the Constitution demands greater specificity of direction than Congress has seen fit to

[87] 315 U.S. 110 (1942).

[88] And see the earlier decision in United States v. Rock Royal Co-op., 307 U.S. 533 (1939).

[89] 317 U.S. 111 (1942).

[90] See also United States v. Appalachian Electric Power Co., 311 U.S. 377 (1940); Oklahoma v. Atkinson, 313 U.S. 508 (1941).

prescribe. But Justice Stone's general appraisal in sustaining the act serves, as always, to state the mood of the evaluation:

> The Constitution, viewed as a continuously operative charter of government, is not to be interpreted as demanding the impossible or the impracticable. The essentials of the legislative function are the determination of the legislative policy and its formulation as a rule of conduct. Those essentials are preserved when Congress specifies the basic conclusions of fact upon ascertainment of which, from relevant data by a designated administrative agency, it ordains that its statutory command is to be effective.[91]

An inquiry conducted in these terms is unlikely to thwart the attainment of congressional objectives by demanding more particular prescription of standards than the subject of the regulation allows. If demonstration were needed it would suffice to point to Chief Justice Stone's opinion sustaining the Price Control Act.[92]

A similar advance towards flexibility was made in dealing with public utility rates. Writing for the Court in *Federal Power Commission v. Natural Gas Pipeline Co.*,[93] Chief Justice Stone affirmed that the "Constitution does not bind rate-making bodies to the service of any single formula or combination of formulas." They are free to make the "pragmatic adjustments which may be called for by particular circumstances." So long as they act within the scope of their statutory authority and their order "as applied to the facts" and "viewed in its entirety, produces no arbitrary result," the judicial "inquiry is at an end."[94]

[91] Opp Cotton Mills v. Administrator, 312 U.S. 126, 145 (1941).
[92] Yakus v. United States, 321 U.S. 414 (1944).
[93] 315 U.S. 575 (1944).
[94] *Id.* at 586. See also Federal Power Commission v. Hope Natural Gas

It has been said, and with obvious force, that in these and related decisions the Court has withdrawn from any significant review of congressional action in the economic field; that apart from areas to be noted hereafter, there has been similar withdrawal in reviewing the action of the states. We may suspect that Justice Stone would have been dissatisfied with a perception that saw no more than a judicial retreat. It would be more faithful to his basic thinking to locate the redefinition in the interpretation of the substantive provisions of the Constitution rather than in the duty of the Court to carry them into effect.[95] And the new definition, he would have been insistent to add, was far more faithful in the large to the historic conception of those provisions than the relatively modern limiting interpretations that he participated in sweeping away. It is in these terms that we must understand the sustained effort in his opinions to recapitulate earlier decisions, the frequent repetition of Marshall's general principles of constitutional exposition, the constant effort to show that in assimilating the "pressing demands of new facts,"[96] continuity was not being lost. He would have been the last to deny that the Court was effecting "the reasonable accommodation of the law to chang-

Co., 320 U.S. 591 (1944). For Justice Stone's earlier views on the scope of due process in rate making, see United Fuel Gas Co. v. Railroad Comm., 278 U.S. 300 (1929); West Ohio Gas Co. v. Public Utilities Comm., 294 U.S. 63, 77 (1935) (concurring); West v. Chesapeake & Potomac Tel. Co., 295 U.S. 662, 680 (1935) (dissent); Northwestern Bell Tel. Co. v. Nebraska State Ry. Comm., 297 U.S. 471 (1936).

95 There may be point, in this context, to Justice Stone's careful affirmation in United States v. Carolene Products Co., 304 U.S. 144 (1938), that the commerce power is limited by the due process clause of the fifth amendment and his invitation of evidence on the issue at the same time that he defined the scope of the power in terms that evidence could hardly meet. And see Federal Power Commission v. Natural Gas Pipe Line Co., 315 U.S. 575 (1944).

96 See Proceedings in Memory of Mr. Justice Brandeis, 317 U.S. ix, xlvi (1942).

ing social and economic needs"[97] but the first to insist that the accommodation was taking place, in an important and meaningful sense, within the framework of the Constitution and in consonance with its basic terms.

To find practical manifestation of this insistence on continuity, we need look no further than Justice Stone's dissent in the *South-Eastern Underwriters* case[98] at the 1943 term. He did not believe that Congress, in enacting the Sherman Act, intended to reach restraints in the execution of contracts of insurance. But he was not content to rest his vote on this ground alone for he saw merit in the traditional doctrine that the execution of the contract itself was not interstate commerce, even though commerce was employed. In "view of the broad powers of the federal government to regulate matters which, though not themselves commerce, nevertheless affect commerce" his position did not deny "the power of Congress if it so desires to regulate many aspects of the insurance business"[99] covered by the indictment. Indeed, he concurred in a decision on the same day sustaining the application of the National Labor Relations Act to an insurance company.[100] But his position did deny the applicability of a statute the terms of which required that commerce be the precise object of the restraint rather than that it be more remotely affected or involved. And not the least of the considerations he advanced in support of his view was also a point of continuity, his fear that the decision would cast a shadow on phases of state regulation which Congress had taken no action to supersede.[101]

97 *Ibid.*
98 United States v. South-Eastern Underwriters Ass'n, 322 U.S. 533 (1944).
99 *Id.* at 580.
100 Polish Alliance v. Labor Board, 322 U.S. 643 (1944).
101 *Cf.* Stone, J., dissenting in *Hines v. Davidowitz*, 312 U.S. 52, 74 (1941):

Invigoration of the commerce and fiscal powers of the Congress resolved fighting issues of transcendent importance to the country and the Court. But the congressional power to govern received sustenance at the hands of Justice Stone in other fields as well. *United States v. Classic*[102] at the 1941 term dispelled the grave doubt engendered by *Newberry v. United States*[103] as to the power of Congress to reach abuses in federal primaries — specifically, the denial of the right of a qualified elector to vote. In finding constitutional sanction for the voter's right when the primary is decisive of the ultimate election the foundation was laid, as the Court held thereafter in *Smith v. Allwright*,[104] for overruling the doctrine of *Grovey v. Townsend*[105] that the fourteenth and fifteenth amendments are inapplicable to racial disqualification for voting when the primary is conducted by a party without explicit authority from the state. Thus the franchise and the congressional power to protect it were both strengthened at the same time.

The war years brought new issues but the direction was generally the same. National price control was sustained, as

"Undoubtedly Congress, in the exercise of its power to legislate in aid of powers granted by the Constitution to the national government may greatly enlarge the exercise of federal authority and to an extent which need not now be defined, it may, if such is its will, thus subtract from the powers which might otherwise be exercised by the states. . . .

"At a time when the exercise of the federal power is being rapidly expanded through Congressional action, it is difficult to overstate the importance of safeguarding against such diminution of state power by vague inferences as to what Congress might have intended if it had considered the matter or by reference to our own conceptions of a policy which Congress has not expressed and which is not plainly to be inferred from the legislation which it has enacted."

See also in this connection Apex Hosiery Co. v. Leader, 310 U.S. 469, 513 (1940); Parker v. Brown, 317 U.S. 341 (1943); Penn Dairies v. Milk Control Commission, 318 U.S. 261 (1943); Borden v. Borella, 325 U.S. 679, 685 (1945) (dissent); Hill v. Florida, 325 U.S. 538, 544 (1945) (concurring).

102 313 U.S. 299 (1941).

103 256 U.S. 232 (1921).

104 321 U.S. 649 (1944).

105 295 U.S. 45 (1935).

was to be expected, the opinion by Chief Justice Stone concerned primarily with the validity of the delegation and the procedural provisions barring attack upon a regulation unless presented in the Emergency Court.[106] The Chief Justice wrote the initial opinion of the Court affirming the awesome sweep of the war power[107] and, having sustained the discriminatory curfew, he concurred thereafter in upholding the evacuation of Japanese Americans from the west coast, decreed by military order supported by congressional and presidential sanction alike.[108] He also wrote for the Court in the *Quirin*[109] case and again at the 1945 term in the case of *Yamashita*[110] upholding the trial of belligerents by military tribunals for offenses under the laws of war. These were the only issues precipitated by the war where resolution was on constitutional grounds.[111]

In finding the central meaning of this chapter of judicial history in the vindication of the power to govern, I have not overlooked the fact that a large part of the issue was framed in terms of the distribution of power between the nation and the states. But the essence of the view which gained dominance in the course of the development is that, whatever the form of the question, when the representatives of the people of all the states deem national rather than local action desirable, it is the power to govern effectively that is almost certainly involved. That this was Justice Stone's belief, his judicial action clearly reveals.

106 Yakus v. United States, 321 U.S. 414 (1944).
107 Hirabayashi v. United States, 320 U.S. 81 (1943).
108 Korematsu v. United States, 323 U.S. 214 (1944).
109 *Ex parte* Quirin, 317 U.S. 1 (1942).
110 327 U.S. 1 (1946).
111 In *Ex parte* Endo, 323 U.S. 283 (1944) (sustaining a petition for writ of habeas corpus filed by a Japanese American in a War Relocation Center), and in Duncan v. Kahanamoku, 327 U.S. 304 (1946) (invalidating military trial of civilians in Hawaii), the Chief Justice concurred in resting decision on the want of statutory authority, without reaching the constitutional issues.

III. The Federal System

Issues of a different order are presented when the Court measures the validity of state action by the postulates of a federal system or the impact of local affirmation on the realization of national aims. The vehicles of adjudication are, of course, the commerce clause, the guarantee of full faith and credit and the due process clause of the fourteenth amendment. Viewed in the large, the question in this area is not whether a legislature has the power to govern but in which legislature the power resides. To reduce the problem to these terms was, at least, one of the dominant objects of Justice Stone's undertaking; and the subject is one with which a large proportion of his effort was concerned.[112]

Jurisdiction

Questions of the jurisdiction of the states in relation to one another call inescapably for arbitral determination if the national authority is to provide in interstate relations a substitute for the diplomatic representation of citizens abroad. What is involved is indeed an aspect of the concern that led the framers to vest original jurisdiction in suits between states in the Supreme Court.[113] While Justice Stone had occasion to affirm that the limits of jurisdiction were exceeded,[114] the major im-

112 See Cheatham, *Stone on Conflict of Laws*, 46 Colum. L. Rev. 719 (1946); Magill, *Stone on Taxation*, *Id.* at 747.

113 *Cf.* Stone, *supra* note 7, at 261–62.

114 See Connecticut General Life Ins. Co. v. Johnson, 303 U.S. 77 (1938) and his concurring opinions in Safe Deposit & Trust Co. v. Virginia, 280 U.S. 83, 85 (1929); and Farmers Loan & Trust Co. v. Minnesota, 280 U.S. 204, 214 (1930).

pact of his opinions and his especial contribution inhered in enlarging the bases upon which jurisdiction is maintained.[115] Here, as in the due process field generally, he fought the battle against constricting limitations, insistent that the issue was solely the question of power; that where local interest provided a basis for action, the prevention of inequity in the impact of legislation was not, as such, the business of the Court.[116] In the field of taxation especially he implemented this conception with all the art of juristic analysis, pushing aside question-begging reifications to reach what he thought the only relevant question, whether the state has conferred any benefits to bottom its demand of a tax. The measure of his triumph in prevailing decisions of the Court is the stubbornness of the effort of some of his brethren to avert double taxation before his position prevailed. In addition to his service in nourishing the power of the states to levy taxes, Justice Stone found means in

[115] *As to taxes,* see Baldwin v. Missouri, 281 U.S. 586, 596 (1930) (dissent); Susquehanna Power Co. v. State Tax Commission, 283 U.S. 297 (1931); First National Bank of Boston v. Maine, 284 U.S. 312, 331 (1932) (dissent); Senior v. Braden, 295 U.S. 422, 433 (1935) (dissent); New York *ex rel.* Cohn v. Graves, 300 U.S. 308 (1937); First Bank Stock Corp. v. Minnesota, 301 U.S. 234 (1937); Curry v. McCanless, 307 U.S. 357 (1939); Graves v. Elliott, 307 U.S. 383 (1939); Pearson v. McGraw, 308 U.S. 313, 319 (1939) (concurring); Graves v. Schmidlapp, 315 U.S. 657 (1942); International Harvester Co. v. Wisconsin, 322 U.S. 435 (1944); *cf.* Tax Commission v. Aldrich, 316 U.S. 174 (1942) (opinion by Douglas, J.).

As to workmen's compensation, see Alaska Packers Ass'n v. Industrial Accident Comm., 294 U.S. 532 (1935); Pacific Employer's Ins. Co. v. Industrial Accident Comm., 306 U.S. 493 (1939); *cf.* Magnolia Petroleum Co. v. Hunt, 320 U.S. 430 (1943).

As to jurisdiction of courts: International Shoe Co. v. Washington, 326 U.S. 310 (1945).

[116] In measuring the jurisdiction of courts over out-of-state parties he did believe, however, that "traditional notions of fair play and substantial justice" have an important place. International Shoe Co. v. Washington, *supra* note 115; and see Pink v. A. A. A. Highway Express Co., 314 U.S. 201 (1941); Riley v. N. Y. Trust Co., 315 U.S. 343, 355 (1942) (concurring).

the Constitution to assist in their collection when it is necessary to reach beyond the taxing state.[117]

Commerce

In dealing with questions of jurisdiction alone, Justice Stone saw no ground for judicial concern that parties with multiple state interests might be subjected to a heavier burden than those with interests in a single state, as in the case of double taxation; or that "the political restraints which are normally exerted on legislation where it affects adversely some interests within the state"[118] might not be expected to operate fully as to them. The ultimate effect of state action upon a just or coherent ordering of rights and duties, measured in national terms, does not encounter anything in the Constitution and, therefore, is not a problem for the Court — except in so far as the states themselves may invoke the original jurisdiction of the Court to litigate a pecuniary interest.[119] A different situation is presented, however, when interstate commerce is involved. Whatever view one may take of the historic debate that began when the framers left off, all must agree that the commerce clause had for its purpose to break down barriers to interstate trade. In this authentic objective Justice Stone perceived the basis for a more positive judicial role.

It will summarize his basic conception to say that as the issues were framed in the long debate the position taken by the Court in *Cooley v. Board of Wardens*[120] comes closest to according with his thought. In his earliest opinions, dealing with both regulation and taxation, he protested what seemed

[117] Milwaukee County v. M. E. White Co., 296 U.S. 268 (1935).

[118] See, *e.g.*, South Carolina State Highway Dep't v. Barnwell Brothers, 303 U.S. 177, 185 (1938); *infra* note 129.

[119] Texas v. Florida, 306 U.S. 398 (1939).

[120] 53 U.S. (12 How.) 299 (1851); *cf.* FRANKFURTER, THE COMMERCE CLAUSE (1937); Dowling, *Interstate Commerce and State Power* (1940) 27 VA. L. REV. 1 (1940).

to him excessive interference with action by the states casting some burden on interstate commerce but protecting interests of legitimate local concern. Moreover, as a solid logician he was offended both by the vacuity of the labels mouthed in the opinions[121] and the emptiness of distinctions taken in the tax cases when measured by the kind of analysis that seemed to him the beginning of thought.[122] Voicing this general critique in his first years Justice Stone was content for a while to manipulate the formulae[123] but in his later opinions he broke new theoretical ground.

[121] *Cf.* his dissent in Di Santo v. Pennsylvania, 273 U.S. 34, 44 (1927) (invalidating as a burden on foreign commerce a state statute requiring licenses of dealers in steamship tickets for foreign travel).

"The recognition of the power of the states to regulate commerce within certain limits is a recognition that there are matters of local concern which may properly be subject to state regulation and which, because of their local character, as well as their number and diversity, can never be adequately dealt with by Congress. Such regulation, so long as it does not impede the free flow of commerce, may properly be and for the most part has been left to the states by the decisions of this Court.

"In this case the traditional test of the limit of state action by inquiring whether the interference with commerce is direct or indirect seems to me too mechanical, too uncertain in its application, and too remote from actualities, to be of value. In thus making use of the expressions 'direct' and 'indirect interference' with commerce, we are doing little more than using labels to describe a result rather than any trustworthy formula by which it is reached."

The *Di Santo* decision was overruled by the Court, in opinion by Mr. Justice Stone, in California v. Thompson, 313 U.S. 109 (1941).

[122] *Cf.* Helson and Randolph v. Kentucky, 279 U.S. 245, 252–253 (1929): "In view of earlier decisions of the Court, I acquiesce in the result. But I cannot yield assent to the reasoning by which the present forbidden tax on the use of property in interstate commerce is distinguished from a permissible tax on property, measured by its use or use value in interstate commerce. . . . Nor can I find any practical justification for this distinction or for an interpretation of the commerce clause which would relieve those engaged in interstate commerce from their fair share of the expense of government of the states in which they operate by exempting them from the payment of a tax of general application, which is neither aimed at nor discriminates against interstate commerce."

[123] See Interstate Busses Corp. v. Blodgett, 276 U.S. 245 (1928) (tax on use of state highways); Boston and Maine R. R. v. Armburg, 285 U.S. 234

The net effect of his view on taxation was that the Court is obliged to protect interstate commerce against discrimination or, what is really the same thing, against state taxes so susceptible of duplication among the several states involved that commerce would be placed at a substantial disadvantage in competition with enterprise operating wholly intrastate. Beyond this, interstate commerce must pay its way and must yield return for services rendered or even for the problems it specially creates.[124] Thus he sustained against bitter opposition the application of a general sales tax to the purchaser in an interstate sale, the seller being obliged to collect and pay,[125] while he adhered to his general condemnation of taxes on gross receipts from activities interstate.[126] He made a different judgment as to the total effect of the two taxes, though it is possible that he anticipated that the invalidity of the one would suffice to avoid a multiple burden from attaching to interstate

(1932) (application of state compensation act to employee of interstate carrier injured while working in intrastate commerce); Nashville C. & St. L. Ry. v. Wallace, 288 U.S. 249 (1933) (tax on storage and withdrawal of gasoline purchased outside state and held for interstate use in normal course); Edelman v. Boeing Air Transport, Inc., 289 U.S. 249 (1933) (same); Federal Compress & Warehouse Co. v. McLean, 291 U.S. 17 (1934) (tax on compressing and warehousing of cotton applied when destined for movement interstate); Clyde Mallory Lines v. Alabama, 296 U.S. 261 (1935) (harbor fee); Fisher's Blend Station v. Tax Commission, 297 U.S. 650 (1936) (tax on gross receipts of radio station broadcasting advertisers' programs interstate); Morf v. Bingaman, 298 U.S. 407 (1936) (reasonable fee for use of roads by cars moving in caravans through the state for sale); Ingels v. Morf, 300 U.S. 290 (1937) (excessive fee for policing caravans).

124 See, in addition to cases cited *supra* note 123, Clark v. Paul Gray, Inc. 306 U.S. 583 (1939); McCarroll v. Dixie Greyhound Lines, 309 U.S. 176, 180 (1940) (concurring); *cf.* Jones v. Opelika, 316 U.S. 584, 600 (1942) (dissent).

125 McGoldrick v. Berwind-White Coal Mining Co., 309 U.S. 33 (1940).

126 Western Livestock v. Bureau of Revenue, 303 U.S. 250, 255–256 (1938); Gwinn, White & Prince, Inc. v. Henneford, 305 U.S. 434 (1939); see also Adams Mfg. Co. v. Storen, 304 U.S. 307 (1938) in which he joined in the opinion of Roberts, J.; *cf.* Northwest Airlines v. Minnesota, 322 U.S. 292, 308 (1944) (dissent).

as opposed to intrastate sales.[127] "Experience has taught," he admonished, "that the opposing demands that the commerce shall bear its share of local taxation, and that it shall not, on the other hand, be subjected to multiple tax burdens merely because it is interstate commerce, are not capable of reconciliation by resort to the syllogism. Practical rather than logical distinctions must be sought."[128]

In the field of regulation Justice Stone was acutely conscious of the manifold ways in which local interests may be imperiled by commerce, whether or not it is interstate. He realized that the problems thus presented call for diversity of solution and could not practically receive attention at all if only the Congress were competent to act.[129] He had seen how judges generally antipathetic to regulation had used the commerce clause to strike down state legislation legitimately protective of such local interests; and he was alert to achieve the opposite result even though some burden might be cast on the commerce that is interstate. So long as the local affirmation bears with relative equality on both domestic and foreign activity with the result that the former would be as eager as the latter to protest any excess or abuse, he thought national commerce adequately protected by its vicarious representation in the political processes of the state.[130] Thus, given a determina-

[127] *Cf.* McLeod v. Dilworth Co., 322 U.S. 327 (1944); General Trading Co. v. Tax Commission, 322 U.S. 335 (1944); Harvester v. Dep't of Treasury, 322 U.S. 340 (1944).

[128] Western Live Stock v. Bureau of Revenue, 303 U.S. 250, 259 (1938). *Cf.* Hooven & Allison Co. v. Evatt, 324 U.S. 652 (1945) presenting the special problem of the scope of the prohibition of state duties on imports. For its solution Chief Justice Stone employed the original package doctrine.

[129] See note 123 *supra;* South Carolina State Highway Dep't v. Barnwell Bros., 303 U.S. 177, 185 (1938); Maurer v. Hamilton, 309 U.S. 598 (1940); Duckworth v. Arkansas, 314 U.S. 390 (1941); Parker v. Brown, 317 U.S. 341 (1943).

[130] See South Carolina State Highway Dep't v. Barnwell Bros., 303 U.S.

tion of the legitimacy of the local interest, as, for example, the maintenance and safety of state highways, he thought the adaptation of the means to the end a legislative rather than a judicial question; it is enough that the legislative method is not "without rational basis."[131]

Reading the *Barnwell* case in 1938 it might have been thought that once a significant local interest was established and the protective measure not shown to lack basis in reason, the judicial task was at an end. Later decisions make clear that this interpretation accords inadequate attention to the equally important insistence that the activity be one which lends itself to diversity in the type of regulation in question, without imperiling unduly the national interest in the flow of commerce and the uniformity of governing standard which contributes to that end. The necessary "accommodation of the state and national interests involved" poses an issue to be determined by the Court "upon a consideration of all the relevant facts and circumstances."[132] That Justice Stone envisaged

177, 187 (1938): "The present regulations, or any others of like purpose, if they are to accomplish their end, must be applied alike to interstate and intrastate traffic both moving in large volume over the highways. The fact that they affect alike shippers in interstate and intrastate commerce in large number within as well as without the state is a safeguard against their abuse." And see *id.* at 184–185, n. 2; McGoldrick v. Berwind-White Coal Mining Co., 309 U.S. 33, 45–46, n. 2 (1940).

[131] South Carolina State Highway Dep't v. Barnwell Bros., 303 U.S. 177, 192 (1938); see also Clark v. Paul Gray, Inc., 306 U.S. 583, 594 (1939). On the interpretation of federal legislation to determine the compatibility of state action when the latter does not plainly conflict, see note 101 *supra;* Maurer v. Hamilton, 309 U.S. 598 (1940); Parker v. Brown 317 U.S. 341 (1943); Southern Pacific Co. v. Arizona, 325 U.S. 761 (1945). *But cf.* Illinois Natural Gas Co. v. Central Illinois Public Serv. Co., 314 U.S. 498 (1942); Davis v. Dep't of Labor, 317 U.S. 249, 260 (1942) (dissent). On the interpretation of a treaty in such circumstances, see Neilsen v. Johnson, 279 U.S. 47 (1929).

[132] Parker v. Brown, 317 U.S. 341, 362 (1943) (sustaining a California marketing program for the raisin crop having the effect of limiting the supply and raising the price of raisins destined for the interstate market, the

this as a tough-minded inquiry is shown clearly enough by one of his last opinions on the subject.

In *Southern Pacific Co. v. Arizona*[133] he spoke for the Court in striking down Arizona's statute limiting the length of railroad trains operated within the state. The act was passed in the view that train lengths in excess of those allowed were conducive to railroad accidents because of the resulting increase of "slack action" of the train. Its effect was to increase substantially the cost of interstate carriage and to delay interstate trains while greater lengths, sanctioned in other states, were reduced at the Arizona border. This burdensome effect was, moreover, potentially subject to duplication since if one state may prescribe a length "so may all the others, and they need not prescribe the same maximum limitation."[134] In addition, the evidence at the trial — which the Court undertook to weigh — showed that the Arizona law was productive rather than preventive of accident, because any safety gain incident to reduced slack was more than offset by the safety loss incident to the increased number of trains.[135] Lacking value as a safety measure, the claim adduced in its support, there was nothing to justify diversity in the limitation of train lengths and its adverse effect on "the interest of the nation in an adequate, economical, and efficient railway transportation

policy of the program coinciding with that of Congress in related agricultural fields).

133 325 U.S. 761 (1945). Justices Black and Douglas dissented.

134 *Id.* at 775.

135 *Id.* at 770–771: "[T]he matters for ultimate determination here are the nature and extent of the burden which the state regulation of interstate trains, adopted as a safety measure, imposes on interstate commerce, and whether the relative weights of the state and national interests involved are such as to make inapplicable the rule, generally observed, that the free flow of interstate commerce and its freedom from local restraints in matters requiring uniformity of regulation are interests safeguarded by the commerce clause from state interference."

service."[136] The marginal judicial review in the case of state highway safety measures, under which the Arizona law would clearly have been sustained, was explained by the peculiarly great local concern in the highways and the fact that their regulation affects large numbers of shippers within as well as without the state.

The residuum of control of state action that Justice Stone reserved for the Court under the commerce clause poses frankly political questions, as Justice Black has emphatically pointed out.[137] But the Court's answers to these questions, though they may rest on the Constitution,[138] have an unusual status. Whenever the Court strikes down state action its judgment is one that the Congress can revise, exercising the grant of power that the commerce clause contains. The revision may be exercised, moreover, not only in relation to particular problems but presumably by general redefinition of the area of forbidden state action that the Court has undertaken to define.[139] Absent congressional action, however, the

[136] *Id.* at 783–784.

[137] *See* Southern Pacific Co. v. Arizona, 325 U.S. 761, 789 (1945); Gwinn, White & Prince, Inc. v. Henneford, 305 U.S. 434, 449 (1939); *cf.* Black, Frankfurter and Douglas, JJ., dissenting in McCarroll v. Dixie Greyhound Lines, 309 U.S. 176, 189 (1940).

[138] Professor Dowling has suggested that the Court's action when Congress has not spoken should be based on a presumed Congressional intention. *Supra* note 120. But Chief Justice Stone declined to be tempted by the theory, asserting only that the "result is the same." Southern Pacific Co. v. Arizona, 325 U.S. 761, 768 (1945).

[139] *Cf.* Southern Pacific Co. v. Arizona, 325 U.S. 761, 769 (1945):

"Congress has undoubted power to redefine the distribution of power over interstate commerce. It may either permit the states to regulate the commerce in a manner which would otherwise not be permissible . . . or exclude state regulation even of matters of peculiarly local concern which nevertheless affect interstate commerce. . . .

"But in general Congress has left it to the courts to formulate the rules thus interpreting the commerce clause in its application, doubtless because it has appreciated the destructive consequences to the commerce of the

function must be performed either by the Court or by the state legislatures. On this score Justice Stone had no doubt where the greater competence to protect the national interest resides. He perceived an opportunity, therefore, for the Court to contribute to government while leaving the legislative power to govern genuinely unimpaired.

Immunity

A somewhat similar direction is evinced in Justice Stone's thinking in the governmental immunity field, where he did so much to shift prevailing doctrine in the Court.[140] The principle laid down by Marshall in *McCulloch v. Maryland*[141] was rendered symmetrical, to the dissent of Justice Bradley, in *Collector v. Day*.[142] Thus developed, the doctrine held that by implication from the structure of the Constitution the nation and its instrumentalities and the states and theirs were reciprocally immune to taxation. The dogma of immunity was to reach the apex of inflation in the early years of Justice Stone's service with a majority holding that royalties from the use of a patent are constitutionally exempt from a general state income tax because the patent is a federal grant.[143] In a

nation if their protection were withdrawn. . . . and has been aware that in their application state laws will not be invalidated without the support of relevant factual material which will 'afford a sure basis' for an informed judgment. . . . Meanwhile, Congress has accommodated its legislation, as have the states, to these rules as an established feature of our constitutional system." See also International Shoe Co. v. Washington, 326 U.S. 310, 315 (1945); Prudential Ins. Co. v. Benjamin, 328 U.S. 408 (1946).

140 See generally T. R. Powell, *The Waning of Intergovernmental Tax Immunities* 58 HARV. L. REV. 633 (1945); *The Remnant of Intergovernmental Tax Immunities* 58 HARV. L. REV. 757 (1945); *cf.* KONEFSKY, *op. cit. supra* note 4, 5–47.

141 17 U.S. (4 Wheat) 316 (1819).

142 78 U.S. (11 Wall) 113 (1871).

143 Long v. Rockwood, 277 U.S. 142 (1927), overruled in Fox Film Corp. v. Doyal, 286 U.S. 123 (1932).

series of well-known cases Justice Stone sought to restate the principle in terms of a practical purpose[144] at the same time that he limited its application as particular situations arose.[145] As in so many other phases of the work of his first ten years, the impact of his judgment was to modify an extreme position which operated as an onerous limitation on the governing power of both the nation and the states.[146]

144 See, *e.g.*, Metcalf & Eddy v. Mitchell, 269 U.S. 514, 523–524 (1926): "... The burden of federal taxation necessarily sets an economic limit to the practical operation of the taxing power of the states, and *vice versa*. Taxation by either the state or the federal government affects in some measure the cost of operation of the other.

"But neither government may destroy the other nor curtail in any substantial manner the exercise of its powers. Hence the limitation upon the taxing power of each, so far as it affects the other, must receive a practical construction which permits both to function with the minimum of interference each with the other; and that limitation cannot be so varied or extended as seriously to impair either the taxing power of the government imposing the tax . . . or the appropriate exercise of the functions of the government affected by it."

145 Metcalf & Eddy v. Mitchell, 269 U.S. 514 (1926); Shaw v. Gibson-Zahneiser Oil Corp., 276 U.S. 575 (1928); National Life Ins. Co. v. United States, 277 U.S. 508, 535 (1928) (dissent); Macallen v. Massachusetts, 279 U.S. 620, 634 (1929) (dissent); Missouri *ex rel.* Missouri Ins. Co. v. Gehner, 281 U.S. 313, 322 (1930) (dissent); Educational Films Corp. v. Ward, 282 U.S. 379 (1931); Group No. 1 Oil Corp. v. Bass, 283 U.S. 279 (1931); Susquehanna Power Co. v. State Tax Commission, 283 U.S. 291 (1931); Indian Motocycle Co. v. United States, 283 U.S. 570, 580 (1931) (dissent); Burnet v. Coronado Oil & Gas Co., 285 U.S. 393, 401 (1932) (dissent); Pacific Co., Ltd. v. Johnson, 285 U.S. 480 (1932); *cf.* Oklahoma Tax Commission v. Barnsdall Refineries, Inc., 296 U.S. 521 (1936); Brush v. Commissioner, 300 U.S. 352, 374 (1937).

146 For illustration of the shrewdness of his method as well as of his ultimate success, see the avoidance of Gillespie v. Oklahoma, 257 U.S. 501 (1922), in Group No. 1 Oil Corp. v. Bass, 283 U.S. 279 (1931), followed by insistence in Burnet v. Coronado Oil & Gas Co., 285 U.S. 393 (1932), that the decisions were inconsistent and that the *Gillespie* case should be overruled, as it ultimately was along with the *Burnet* case in Helvering v. Mountain Producers Corp., 303 U.S. 376 (1938). For similar developments see Macallen v. Massachusetts, 279 U.S. 620 (1929); Educational Films Corp. v. Ward 282 U.S. 379 (1931); and Pacific Co., Ltd. v. Johnson, 285 U.S. 480 (1932); or the success of the dissent in Indian Motocycle Co. v. United

In 1938, the same year that he undertook to redefine the governing formulae in commerce cases,[147] Justice Stone passed beyond the plea that the immunity should not be extended[148] and substantially curtailed its previously acknowledged scope. *Helvering v. Gerhardt*[149] greatly narrowed the immunity of the salaries of state employees and *Graves v. O'Keefe*,[150] the next year, made a clean sweep denying protection to government officers or employees whether in the service of nation or state. In the application to government personnel of the income tax exacted from everyone else, Justice Stone saw no threat to the employing sovereignty; nor did he perceive in the conjectural necessity of increasing government salaries an economic burden comparable in significance to the impairment of the power to tax. That the uncertainty of the economic burden was not of the essence of the decisions was made clear two years later in sustaining a state tax on a purchase by a cost plus contractor, constituting an expense which the United States was contractually obligated to defray.[151]

States, 283 U.S. 570, 580 (1931), in James v. Dravo Contracting Co., 302 U.S. 134, 151 (1937), and Alabama v. King & Boozer, 314 U.S. 1 (1941), overruling Panhandle Oil Co. v. Knox, 277 U.S. 218 (1928), the object of the original attack.

147 *Supra*, pp. 117–118.

148 Indian Motocycle v. United States, 283 U.S. 570, 580 (1931): "The implied immunity of one government, either national or state, from taxation by the other should not be enlarged. Immunity of the one necessarily involves curtailment of the other's sovereign power to tax. The practical effect of enlargement is commonly to relieve individuals from a tax, at the expense of the government imposing it, without substantial benefit to the government for whose theoretical advantage the immunity is invoked."

149 304 U.S. 405 (1938).

150 306 U.S. 466 (1939).

151 Alabama v. King & Boozer, 314 U.S. 1, 8–9 (1941): "So far as such a non-discriminatory state tax upon the contractor enters into the cost of materials to the Government, that is but a normal incident of the organization within the same territory of two independent taxing sovereignties." See also Wilson v. Cook, 327 U.S. 499 (1946); Superior Bath House Co. v. McCarroll, 312 U.S. 176, 181 (1941) (concurring).

Whether the same result will be reached in the case of government bonds only the future can tell.

These contractions of the area of immunity applied equally whether the government affected was federal or state. In the opinions in the salary cases, however, Justice Stone re-examined the doctrine that the immunities have reciprocal scope. Building on a passage in *McCulloch v. Maryland*[152] he reminds us that

> the people of all the states have created the national government and are represented in Congress. Through that representation they exercise the national taxing power. The very fact that when they are exercising it they are taxing themselves, serves to guard against its abuse through the possibility of resort to the usual processes of political action which provides a readier and more adaptable means than any which courts can afford, for securing accommodation of the competing demands for national revenue, on the one hand, and for reasonable scope for the independence of state action, on the other.

On the other hand, if the federal power is once "impaired by the recognition of a state immunity found to be excessive, restoration of that power is not likely to be secured through the action of state legislatures; for they are without the inducements to act which have often persuaded Congress to waive immunities thought to be excessive."[153] It is this distinction which justifies limitation of the immunity, even when the state itself is subjected to a nondiscriminatory tax, to cases where the function taxed is "essential to the maintenance of a

[152] 17 U.S. (4 Wheat.) 316, 435–36 (1819); see also the dissent of Bradley, J., in Collector v. Day, 78 U.S. (11 Wall.) 113, 128 (1871).

[153] Helvering v. Gerhardt, 304 U.S. 405, 416, 417 (1938).

state government"[154] or, as Chief Justice Stone restated it a few months before his death, where the "tax unduly interferes with the performance of the State's functions of government."[155] Here too the "problem is not one to be solved by a formula"; and the "effect of the immunity on the national taxing power is to be determined not quantitatively but by its operation and tendency in withdrawing taxable property or activities from the reach of federal taxation."[156] Thus, however the standard would be applied in difficult cases, there is room for consideration both of the scope of governmental activity in contemplation when the Constitution was adopted and of what may be deemed to be essential to government at any particular time.

If the federal government may tax even the state itself, except in this reserved area, the reciprocal does not ever obtain unless Congress has given its consent. Neither the United States as an entity nor any of the departments or organs of its government nor its property may be subjected to state taxation[157] or indeed to any form of direct state limitation,[158] unless the underlying federal statutes indicate congressional consent.[159] Moreover, Congress may provide a statutory immunity to the extent that such a provision may be thought necessary

[154] *Id.* at 417. See also *id.* at 414: "The immunity . . . was sustained only because it was one deemed necessary to protect the states from destruction by the federal taxation of those governmental functions which they were exercising when the Constitution was adopted and which were essential to their continued existence."

[155] New York v. United States, 326 U.S. 572, 588 (1946).

[156] *Id.* at 590.

[157] See, *e.g.*, United States v. County of Allegheny, 322 U.S. 174 (1944) (opinion by Jackson, J.); S. R. A., Inc. v. Minnesota, 327 U.S. 558, 570 (1946) (concurring).

[158] *cf.* Mayo v. United States, 319 U.S. 441 (1943) (opinion by Reed, J.).

[159] See, *e.g.*, Smith v. Davis, 323 U.S. 111 (1944) (opinion by Murphy, J.); *cf.* R.F.C. v. Menihan Corp., 312 U.S. 81 (1941) (opinion by Hughes, C. J.); Federal Land Bank v. Priddy, 295 U.S. 229 (1935).

or appropriate to protect a federal operation, in the areas where the burden itself would bring no constitutional bar into play[160] — though such an intention is rarely to be implied in the absence of express provision.[161] Thus there is a very extensive difference under the doctrine, as it developed in Justice Stone's thought, between the immunity of the national government and that of the states, a product, of course, of the supremacy of Congress within its authorized field.[162] And the net effect of the development, here as in the case of commerce, is to enhance the state legislative power while extending the power of Congress to resolve the conflicting policies by laying down the governing rule.

IV. The Protected Area of Liberty

We shall distort Justice Stone's participation in the reformulation of constitutional doctrine if we estimate his contribution in terms of the vindication of government alone. For it is the paradox of the period, if paradox it be, that new areas of constitutional protection were emerging even as the power to

[160] See Graves v. New York *ex rel.* O'Keefe, 306 U.S. 466, 478, 479 (1939); Alabama v. King & Boozer, 314 U.S. 1, 8 (1941); James v. Dravo Contracting Co., 302 U.S. 134, 161 (1937); Oklahoma Tax Comm. v. United States, 319 U.S. 598 (1943) (opinion by Black, J.); *cf.* Pittman v. Home Owners' Loan Corp., 308 U.S. 21 (1939) (opinion by Hughes, C. J.).

[161] See, in addition to cases cited *supra* note 160, Stone, C. J., in Penn Dairies, Inc. v. Milk Control Comm., 318 U.S. 261, 274–275 (1943): "Evidence is wanting that Congress, in authorizing competitive bidding, has been so concerned with securing the lowest possible price for articles furnished to the government that it wished to set aside all local regulations affecting price. . . . An unexpressed purpose of Congress to set aside statutes of the states regulating their internal affairs is not lightly to be inferred and ought not to be implied where the legislative command, read in the light of its history, remains ambiguous." *Cf.* notes 101, 131, *supra.*

[162] *Cf.* United States v. California, 297 U.S. 175 (1936), holding the immunity principle inapplicable to limit congressional regulation of interstate commerce.

govern was being sustained. And Justice Stone's part in this branch of the development was no less commanding than in the portion of the story we have told.[163]

The background marks a curious contrast to the fields we have previously explored. The Court that found so much in the Constitution to limit economic regulation read with a less exacting eye the guarantees of the first amendment. As convictions were sustained under the Espionage Act after World War I, it was Justice Holmes and Brandeis whose voices were frequently raised in dissent.[164] Recognizing that freedom of speech and assembly could not be taken as absolute rights, they urged a standard to measure their qualification that would accord them a meaningful scope. "The question in every case," said Justice Holmes, is "whether the words are used in such circumstances and are of such a nature as to create a clear and present danger that they will bring about the substantive evils that Congress has a right to prevent."[165] When the espionage cases had been finished, comparable issues came to the Court from the states. It was then that the Court established that the due process clause of the fourteenth amendment imposed some limitations on the states in relation

[163] I have omitted procedural guarantees from the discussion, despite the importance of their development during the last years, for the impact of Justice Stone's contribution was in the substantive field. But *cf.* Olmstead v. United States, 277 U.S. 438, 488 (1928) (wiretapping; dissent); Husty v. United States, 282 U.S. 694 (1931) (search and seizure); Raffel v. United States, 271 U.S. 494 (1926) (self-incrimination); Hill v. Texas, 316 U.S. 400 (1942) (Negro exclusion from grand jury); *In re* Bradley, 318 U.S. 50, 53 (1943) (dissent); Malinski v. New York, 324 U.S. 401, 434 (1945) (confession; dissent). See also Beazell v. Ohio, 269 U.S. 167 (1925) (ex post facto); Lindsey v. Washington, 301 U.S. 397 (1937) (same); Hansberry v. Lee, 311 U.S. 32 (1940) (*res judicata*); Anderson National Bank v. Luckett, 321 U.S. 233 (1944).

[164] See Abrams v. United States, 250 U.S. 616 (1919); Schaefer v. United States, 251 U.S. 466 (1920); Pierce v. United States, 252 U.S. 239 (1920).

[165] Schenck v. United States, 249 U.S. 47, 52 (1919).

to assembly or speech,[166] a position that Charles Warren epitomized as "The New 'Liberty' Under the Fourteenth Amendment."[167] The protection that the Court afforded was, however, attenuated by the very deference to the judgment embodied in legislation that the dissenters demanded in property cases and the majority of the Court denied.[168] The position was inverted, moreover, on the minority side as well. For as the theory of the dissenters developed it demanded more than that speech be protected unless it creates or is intended to create[169] a "clear and present danger" of some evil that the state may constitutionally undertake to prevent. It asserted that prohibition "of free speech and assembly is a measure so stringent that it would be inappropriate as the means for averting a relatively trivial harm to society"; that "even imminent danger cannot justify resort to prohibition of these functions essential to effective democracy, unless the evil apprehended is relatively serious."[170] It seems clear, as I have elsewhere attempted to show,[171] that the dissenting demand could mean no less than an extended judicial evaluation (in the fullest legislative sense) of the competing values presented in any situation in which it was attempted to limit freedom of speech or assembly for the attainment of some legislative end. It is well to add that in so far as this position was urged by

166 Gitlow v. New York, 268 U.S. 652 (1925); *cf.* Patterson v. Colorado, 205 U.S. 454, 462 (1907).

167 39 HARV. L. REV. 431 (1926).

168 Gitlow v. New York, 268 U.S. 652, 668 (1925); Whitney v. California, 274 U.S. 357 (1927). The presumption did not apply, however, if all that was prohibited was advocacy of peaceful change. See Fiske v. Kansas, 274 U.S. 380 (1927).

169 See Abrams v. United States, 250 U.S. 616, 627, 630 (1919).

170 Brandeis, J., concurring in Whitney v. California, 274 U.S. 357, 377 (1927).

171 *Symposium on Civil Liberties* 9 AMERICAN LAW SCHOOL REV. 881, 887 (1941).

Justice Brandeis under the fourteenth rather than the first amendment, it was premised on the proposition that the Court had definitely rejected arguments which seemed to him "persuasive" that the due process clause embodied procedural protections alone.[172]

At the time of Justice Stone's appointment the espionage cases were at an end; and the *Gitlow* case, having been twice argued, was presumably decided without his vote. In the *Whitney* case, which brought forth Justice Brandeis' great concurring opinion, Justice Stone was content to join in the statement of the Court. And when, in the following years, the judgments of the Court took a position more protective of liberty, the opinions were usually written by Chief Justice Hughes or Justice Roberts;[173] Justice Stone was with them invariably in the voting but he did not state his views.

The first expression of his thought on these issues comes characteristically in a footnote[174] and its concern is the scope of judicial review. The decision affirms the wide latitude of legislative discretion in the case of "regulatory legislation affecting ordinary commercial transactions" and the breadth of the presumption of validity which, as we have said, is its procedural concomitant:

> There may be narrower scope for operation of the presumption of constitutionality when legislation appears on its face to be within a specific prohibition of the Constitution, such as those of the first ten amendments, which are deemed

172 Whitney v. California, 274 U.S. 357, 373 (1927).

173 Stromberg v. California, 283 U.S. 359 (1931); Near v. Minnesota, 283 U.S. 697 (1931); De Jonge v. Oregon, 299 U.S. 353 (1937); Herndon v. Lowry, 301 U.S. 242 (1937); Lovell v. Griffin, 303 U.S. 444 (1938); see also Grosjean v. American Press Co., 297 U.S. 233 (1936).

174 United States v. Carolene Products Co., 304 U.S. 144, 152–153, n. 4 (1938).

equally specific when held to be embraced within the Fourteenth.

And, in the same vein of suggestive conjecture, he carries the thought further:

> It is unnecessary to consider now whether legislation which restricts those political processes which can ordinarily be expected to bring about repeal of undesirable legislation, is to be subjected to more exacting judicial scrutiny under the general prohibitions of the Fourteenth Amendment than are most other types of legislation. . . .
>
> Nor need we enquire whether similar considerations enter into the review of statutes directed at particular religious . . . or national . . . or racial minorities, . . . whether prejudice against discrete and insular minorities may be a special condition, which tends seriously to curtail the operation of those political processes ordinarily to be relied upon to protect minorities, and which may call for a correspondingly more searching judicial inquiry.

If these issues might be reserved in theory, in practice they could not long be postponed. A city ordinance required a permit for meetings in streets or public places which a director of public safety might deny if he thought disorder likely to result. It soon fell under the fourteenth amendment;[175] and in other cases the desire for cleanliness of the thoroughfares was held insufficient to sustain a similar limitation on the distribution of leaflets on the streets.[176] Shortly thereafter, and

175 Hague v. Committee for Industrial Organization, 307 U.S. 496 (1939).

176 Schneider v. State, 308 U.S. 147, 161 (1939) (Roberts, J.): "In every case, therefore, where legislative abridgement of the rights is asserted, the courts should be astute to examine the effect of the challenged legislation. Mere legislative preferences or beliefs respecting matters of public convenience may well support regulation directed at other personal activities,

far more significantly, peaceful picketing was protected as the workman's freedom of speech; the economic disadvantage to the concern picketed was held "neither so serious nor so imminent as to justify the sweeping proscription of freedom" embodied in a statute by which picketing was generally condemned.[177] It was clear by now not only that the first amendment was firmly read into due process of the fourteenth, but, what was far more important, that in this area of conduct the Court was fully prepared to undertake the "more exacting judicial scrutiny" to which Justice Stone had referred. Joining in all these decisions, he wrote only in the *Hague* case; and there the major burden of his opinion was to urge that the constitutional standard be anchored in the due process clause of the fourteenth amendment rather than in the "privileges and immunities" clause which had been quiescent since the adoption of the amendment and applied, in any event, only to citizens of the United States.[178]

At the end of the 1939 term, he undertook to speak at length.[179] Two children, aged twelve and ten, were required by the Board of Education to join teachers and schoolmates in

but be insufficient to justify such as diminishes the exercise of rights so vital to the maintenance of democratic institutions. And so, as cases arise, the delicate and difficult task falls upon the courts to weigh the circumstances and to appraise the substantiality of the reasons advanced in support of the regulation of the free enjoyment of the rights."

177 Thornhill v. Alabama, 310 U.S. 88, 105 (1940); see also Carlson v. California, 310 U.S. 106 (1940); American Federation of Labor v. Swing, 312 U.S. 321 (1941). See Biddle, *Past Term of the Supreme Court of the United States* 4 FED. B. A. J. 218 (1941).

178 307 U.S. 496, 518, 524 (1939): "No more grave and important issue can be brought to this Court than that of freedom of speech and assembly, which the due process clause guarantees to all persons regardless of their citizenship, but which the privileges and immunities clause secures only to citizens, and then only to the limited extent that their relationship to the national government is affected." *Cf.* Colgate v. Harvey, 296 U.S. 404, 436 (1935).

179 Minersville School District v. Gobitis, 310 U.S. 586, 601 (1940) (dissent).

the ceremony of salute to the flag. Members of Jehovah's Witnesses, they refused on religious grounds and were expelled. In a suit for injunction by their father, the Court held that they had no case. "To stigmatize legislative judgment in providing for this universal gesture of respect for the symbol of our national life in the setting of the common school as a lawless inroad on that freedom of conscience which the Constitution protects, would amount to no less than the pronouncement of pedagogical and psychological dogma in a field where courts possess no marked and certainly no controlling competence."[180] In thus deferring to local judgment, Justice Frankfurter wrote for everyone but Justice Stone.

The reply was addressed both to the scope of judicial review in cases of this kind and to the specific issue involved. To defer to legislative judgment in such a situation is "no less than the surrender of the constitutional protection of the liberty of small minorities to the popular will." What is required is "a searching judicial inquiry."[181] Measured in these terms, "the right of this small and helpless minority, including children having a strong religious conviction, whether they understand its nature or not, to refrain from an expression obnoxious to their religion" is not to "be overborne by the interest of the state in maintaining discipline in the schools."[182] Even "if we believe that such compulsions will contribute to national unity, there are other ways to teach loyalty and patriotism which are the sources of national unity, than by compelling the pupil to affirm that which he does not believe and by commanding a form of affirmance which violates his religious convictions."[183] The "very terms of the Bill of Rights preclude . . . any reconciliation of such com-

[180] *Id.* at 597–598. [181] *Id.* at 606.
[182] *Ibid.* [183] *Ibid.* at 603–604.

pulsions with the constitutional guaranties by a legislative declaration that they are more important to the public welfare than the Bill of Rights."[184] The "Constitution expresses more than the conviction of the people that democratic processes must be preserved at all costs. It is also an expression of faith and a command that freedom of mind and spirit must be preserved, which government must obey, if it is to adhere to that justice and moderation without which no free government can exist."[185]

Two years later three of the Justices who concurred in the majority opinion asserted that they had concluded they were wrong;[186] a year after that the views of Justice Stone on the flag-salute had been adopted by a majority of the Court.[187]

The transformation of dissent to judgment was by this time hardly new to Chief Justice Stone but this was the first time that the dissent had been rendered in the new Court. It is striking, moreover, that in this most delicate area of constitutional adjudication, where he expressed his views so rarely, the experience occurred again.[188] And surely it is worthy of note that, controlling the assignment of opinions, when the vindi-

184 *Id.* at 605. 185 *Id.* at 606–607.

186 Black, Douglas and Murphy, J.J., dissenting in Jones v. Opelika, 316 U.S. 584, 623 (1942).

187 Board of Education v. Barnette, 319 U.S. 624 (1943).

188 Jones v. Opelika, 316 U.S. 584, 600 (1942) (dissent), *rehearing granted*, 316 U.S. 649 (1942), *judgment reversed*, 319 U.S. 103 (1943). See also Murdock v. Pennsylvania, 319 U.S. 105 (1943); Martin v. Struthers, 319 U.S. 141 (1943); Douglas v. Jeannette, 319 U.S. 157 (1943). The *Jones* and *Murdock* cases involved license taxes exacted by municipal ordinance as a condition of canvassing or soliciting. They were held invalid as applied to the sale of religious literature by religious colporteurs. See also Follett v. Town of McCormick, 321 U.S. 573 (1944). The *Martin* decision struck down an ordinance forbidding anyone, not specifically invited, to use door bells or summon the occupant of any private residence to the door for the purpose of receiving a handbill, circular, or advertisement as applied to a person distributing advertisements for a religious meeting. The right held infringed was the freedom of speech and the press.

cation came he accorded others the opportunity to state the position of the Court.

In according a "preferred position" to the guarantees of the first amendment and the incorporation of its substance into the due process of the fourteenth,[189] Justice Stone relied essentially on the explicit statement of these freedoms in the Bill of Rights[190] and the spirit of the historic insistence that they be expressly set forth. If the fourteenth amendment guarantees any liberties which can they be if not these? We may be certain, however, that in the final statement, though he pointed to the text, and its logic, and the history that gave it birth, he would not have rested on them alone. Within the discipline of his method and his sense for the demands of continuity, he was reshaping the fundamental law as he believed judges should — in accordance with that "sober second thought of the community, which is the firm base on which all law must ultimately rest."[191] Hence, though he was bold and determined, he was never doctrinaire. The inquiry and the judgment take into account the nature of the issue and the actual stakes involved, according a great but not necessarily dispositive value to the element of freedom impaired.

189 See Stone, J., in Jones v. Opelika, 316 U.S. 584, 608 (1942): "The First Amendment is not confined to safeguarding freedom of speech and freedom of religion against discriminatory attempts to wipe them out. On the contrary, the Constitution, by virtue of the First and the Fourteenth Amendments, has put those freedoms in a preferred position. Their commands are not restricted to cases where the protected privilege is sought out for attack. They extend at least to every form of taxation which, because it is a condition of the exercise of the privilege, is capable of being used to control or suppress it."

190 See Minersville School District v. Gobitis, 310 U.S. 586, 602 (1940) (dissent). "The very fact that we have constitutional guaranties of civil liberties and the specificity of their command where freedom of speech and of religion are concerned require some accommodation of the powers which government normally exercises, when no question of civil liberty is involved, to the constitutional demand that those liberties be protected against the action of government itself."

191 See note 24 *supra*.

We may see this most clearly in the Japanese curfew case, his only other important opinion in this field.[192] The examination extended to "whether in the light of all the facts and circumstances there was any substantial basis for the conclusion, in which Congress and the military commander united, that the curfew as applied was a protective measure necessary to meet the threat of sabotage and espionage which would substantially affect the war effort and which might reasonably be expected to aid a threatened enemy invasion" and whether there was "reasonable ground for believing that the threat" was "real."[193] Concluding that this standard was satisfied, he did not ask in addition whether he would have preferred to take more chances or whether the judgment was the one he would have made. Had the stakes involved been smaller, we may suppose that the inquiry would have been more severe.[194]

Except for one further opinion urging that an alleged misrepresentation of religious experience can be litigated as any other fraud,[195] we may discern the lines Justice Stone was prepared to draw only from the evidence of his votes.

He joined in the judgments holding picketing constitutionally protected even when part of a secondary boycott[196] but not when the grievance was entirely unconnected with the

[192] Hirabayashi v. United States, 320 U.S. 81 (1943); see also Korematsu v. United States, 323 U.S. 214 (1944).

[193] Hirabayashi v. United States, 320 U.S. 81, 95 (1943). See also Duncan v. Kahanomoku, 327 U.S. 304 (1946).

[194] *Cf.* Stone, J., concurring in Skinner v. Oklahoma, 316 U.S. 535, 544 (1942): "There are limits to the extent to which the presumption of constitutionality can be pressed, especially where the liberty of the person is concerned . . . and where the presumption is resorted to only to dispense with a procedure which the ordinary dictates of prudence would seem to demand for the protection of the individual from arbitrary action."

[195] United States v. Ballard, 322 U.S. 78 (1944) (dissent).

[196] Bakery & Pastry Drivers & Helpers Local v. Wohl, 315 U.S. 769 (1942); *cf.* American Federation of Labor v. Swing, 312 U.S. 321 (1941).

operation of the business where the pickets marched.[197] He joined a majority of the Court in sustaining a state injunction against peaceful as well as violent picketing where the background was one of violence found to impute a prospective threat.[198] But he cast his vote with the minority when the Court struck down a state requirement enforced by injunction that labor organizers register, as applied to a labor union officer who came to the state for the purpose of making a speech.[199] He supported the leaflet distributor and the religious colporteur in all the cases in which restrictions were invalidated by the Court on which he sat,[200] except the Witnesses of Jehovah who insisted upon continuing their mission though directed to withdraw from the street of a company[201] and a federal[202] town. He stood with the Court in deciding that in prohibiting child labor a state may forbid the sale of religious pamphlets though done with religious intent.[203] And he joined the dissent in insisting that the interest of a state in the dispassionate administration of justice sustains a power to punish as contempt both a newspaper demand for severe sentence and a threat to call a strike, when intended or reasonably

[197] Carpenters & Joiners Union v. Ritter's Café, 315 U.S. 722 (1942).

[198] Milk Wagon Drivers' Union v. Meadowmoor Dairies, Inc., 312 U.S. 287 (1941); *cf.* Hotel & Restaurant Employees' Local v. Wisconsin Employment Relations Board, 315 U.S. 437 (1942). *But cf.* Cafeteria Employees Union v. Angelos, 320 U.S. 293 (1943).

[199] Thomas v. Collins, 323 U.S. 516 (1945).

[200] See, in addition to cases cited *supra* notes 176, 187, 188; Lovell v. Griffin, 303 U.S. 444 (1938); Cantwell v. Connecticut, 310 U.S. 296 (1940); Jamison v. Texas, 318 U.S. 413 (1943); Largent v. Texas, 318 U.S. 418 (1943). See also Taylor v. Mississippi, 319 U.S. 583 (1943). *But cf.* Cox v. New Hampshire, 312 U.S. 569 (1941); Chaplinsky v. New Hampshire, 315 U.S. 568 (1942).

[201] Marsh v. Alabama, 326 U.S. 501 (1946).

[202] Tucker v. Texas, 326 U.S. 517 (1946).

[203] Prince v. Massachusetts, 321 U.S. 158 (1944).

likely to disturb the placidity of the process of decision in a pending case.[204]

We can not know where Justice Stone would have ultimately drawn the lines in this emerging area of protection, had he remained somewhat longer with the task. But we may judge from the evidence of his labors the governing standard he would have set: to preserve the essentials of freedom without impairing the power to govern. The application of that standard necessarily presents a problem of imposing difficulty. We may hope that those who are responsible for its solution in the future will be as successful in their time as Justice Stone was in his.

[204] Bridges v. California and Times-Mirror Co. v. Superior Court, 314 U.S. 252 (1941); *cf.* Nye v. United States, 313 U.S. 33 (1941).

The Issues of the Nuremberg Trial

ONE may say without impertinence to historians that the judgment that history will render upon a legal proceeding is not usually a matter of acute concern either to counsel or to the court. In this respect, at least, the Nuremberg trial was a highly exceptional affair; for the perspective of most of the participants, and even that of the defendants, was focused very much on the future, distant and problematical as it is. The dominant mood was put in words by Justice Jackson, in opening the case for the prosecution: "We must never forget that the record on which we judge these defendants to-day is the record on which history will judge us to-morrow."[1]

The verdict of history will not be rendered for a long time, but we may be certain that the process of deliberation will be as active as the debate that has been under way. The trial is extolled as a crucial achievement in the development of international law, a triumph of reason and justice in the bitter

NOTE: This paper, with some omission of detail, was read at the Annual Meeting of the American Historical Association, December 30, 1946. It was first published in 62 POL. SCI. Q. 11 (1947).

[1] See 2 INTERNATIONAL MILITARY TRIBUNAL, TRIAL OF THE MAJOR WAR CRIMINALS 101 (Nuremberg, 1947).

wake of the war. But voices have been raised from the beginning to proclaim the battle cry of the attack: novelty and confusion, error and pretense, a peril to essential liberties safeguarded by domestic law. What are the issues that challenge examination as this active critique unfolds? What are the factors to be weighed in the balance by those who will record for the judgment of posterity the history of our turbulent time?

I

It is a lawyer's habit, that I would not resist if I could, to begin with a statement of the case.

Credible information received in the course of the war reported cruelties and atrocities perpetrated by the Germans, especially in the occupied countries, that no conception of military necessity could sustain. Impotent to render physical assistance, the heads of state of the principal Allies responded with warnings, jointly and severally repeated, that the guilty would be apprehended and punished. The triumph of arms brought with it the physical custody of thousands of persons suspected of complicity in the conduct to which these warnings had been addressed. It brought the custody of the survivors among the principal enemy personalities believed, upon probable cause, to be responsible for the initiation of the war. Most of these persons had, indeed, made frantic efforts to surrender to the forces advancing from the west; and by far the largest number when the firing ceased were in American hands. Within Germany no governmental authority survived the unconditional surrender, save that which the Potsdam Powers themselves exercised by the military occupation. It took no great foresight in the last days to anticipate that these conditions would obtain. It was essential that a policy be formulated for dealing with the individuals in question when the fighting should finally come to an end.

The problem thus presented was answered by the principal Allies in the Agreement executed in London on August 8, 1945, to which nineteen other nations thereafter adhered. It is no secret that this protocol represented, in its major content, the proposals put forward by Justice Jackson on behalf of the United States. It provided for the creation of a Tribunal, deemed to exercise military powers and therefore entitled the "International Military Tribunal"; each of the four signatories was to designate one member and an alternate. The Tribunal was accorded jurisdiction "to try and punish persons who, acting in the interests of the European Axis countries," might be charged and convicted of any of the conduct which the Charter defined as a crime. The crimes thus defined were called "crimes against peace," "war crimes," and "crimes against humanity." Crimes against peace comprehended in substance the "planning, preparation, initiation, or waging of a war of aggression, or a war in violation of international treaties . . . or assurances" or conspiring so to do. War crimes comprehended generally "violations of the laws or customs of war" with some specification of the behavior, such as the murder or ill-treatment of prisoners of war, deemed to constitute such violations. The definition of crimes against humanity supplemented that of crimes of war — but the concept was accorded very little scope because of the requirement that the acts of inhumanity included be committed "in execution of or in connection with" some other crime within the jurisdiction of the Tribunal, that is, a crime against peace or a war crime.

For such conduct the Charter declared that "there shall be

individual responsibility"; that "leaders, organizers, instigators, and accomplices" conspiring to commit such offenses were mutually responsible for the actions perpetrated in the execution of their common plan; that official position was neither an excuse nor a mitigation; and that superior orders might be a mitigation if justice so required, but not a defense.

In addition, the Charter provided that in the trial of any individual and in connection with any act of which he might be convicted, the Tribunal might declare that "the group or organization of which the individual was a member was a criminal organization." The point of such a declaration was that thereafter the members of the organization might be prosecuted for their membership in "national, military, or occupation courts" of the signatories — in which event the Charter provided that "the criminal nature of the group or organization is considered proved and shall not be questioned."

These are the substantive provisions of the Charter and they are the only ones which gave rise to any significant problems; for the procedural portion, designed to safeguard the rights of individual defendants and to protect the fairness of the trial, embodied, with small exceptions, the major lessons of civilization in relation to criminal procedure. Representing as they did a combination of the inquisitorial and the accusatorial systems, I put them aside with the assertion that, as implemented by the Nuremberg Tribunal, they included most of the salutary features of each. I wish, indeed, that the average impecunious defendant in an American court could count on assistance as extensive in the preparation and presentation of his defense.

The issues that are important are those presented by the Charter in its substantive aspects, as interpreted and applied by the Nuremberg Court. The Charter was, of course, binding upon the Tribunal in the same way that a constitutional statute would bind a domestic court. But the generalizations set forth in the Agreement demanded, as legislation always does, creative interpretation in its application to the challenging facts of a particular case.

On October 18, 1945, in a reconstruction of the chamber in Berlin where Nazi justice had its last major exhibition, the Tribunal constituted under the Charter held its first public session. Prosecutors representing the United States, the United Kingdom, the Soviet Union, and France filed a joint indictment against Goering and twenty-three others, charging crimes against peace, war crimes, and crimes against humanity, committed pursuant to a conspiracy alleged to be criminal in itself, in the sense that it had or grew to have these criminal ends. The indictment recited in great detail the particulars of the conduct which the defendants were charged with planning and carrying out: the long course of bellicose aggression, the acts of systematic inhumanity — of which simple murder was far from the worst — committed in the preparation and conduct of the war. It specified the alleged complicity of each of the defendants. In addition, it prayed for a declaration that six organizations, the Reich Cabinet, the Leadership Corps of the Nazi Party, the Gestapo (including the S.D.), the S.A., the S.S., and the General Staff and High Command, constituted "criminal organizations."

Twenty-two of the twenty-four individual defendants were brought to trial, one of them, Martin Bormann, *in absentia*. After a trial lasting the better part of a year, on a record exceeding 17,000 pages depicting horrors never before recorded in a court, Schacht, Von Papen, and Fritzsche were acquitted; the declaration of criminality was denied in the case of the Cabinet, the General Staff, and the S.A., and granted, but in highly qualified and limiting terms, with respect to the Leadership Corps, the Gestapo, and the S.S. Nineteen individuals were convicted, of whom eleven, including Bormann, were sentenced to death, the others to imprisonment for terms ranging from ten years to life. All of those sentenced to death were convicted of war crimes or crimes against humanity; all but four, Kaltenbrunner, Frank, Sauckel, and Bormann, were also convicted of crimes against peace.

History will ask whether these men and these organizations were justly condemned or acquitted. The inquiry will involve many phases, not all of which can be examined here. I shall attempt no more than to direct attention to the most important points.

II

Should the United States — and the question may be put with equal validity for each of the victors — have cast its influence against any punitive proceedings, declining to participate and refusing to surrender the persons of its prisoners to other countries clamoring to proceed? Such a course would have forsaken the pledges and the warnings issued as an instrument of war and would have responded with a blanket *nolumus* to the demand for retribution that rose like a plaintive chant from all the desolated lands. Certainly only the firmest conviction that punishment in this situation could serve no adequate temporal purpose would have sanctioned dismissal of the millions of complainants with the admonition that "vengeance belongs to God." In truth, the volume of accumulated passion sufficed in itself to establish such a temporal purpose — for who can doubt that indiscriminate violence, a blood bath beyond power of control, would have followed an announcement by the responsible governments that they were unwilling to proceed? If nothing else was to be accomplished, it was essential that some institutional mechanism be provided that would reserve the application of violence to the public force, to cases in which punishment might serve a constructive purpose and in which reason would conclude that it was deserved.

It is not to be conceded, however, that this negative function, whatever its importance, is the only purpose that was to be served. The assumption of domestic society that punishment is a preventive weapon is not as irrelevant to international behavior as some persons seem disposed to affirm. In so far as the penalty eliminates a danger presented by the particular individual — hardly an objective of indifference to a military occupation — the function is no less plain in this situation than it is in municipal affairs. But the dominant justification of punishment, especially of the punishment of death, is usually felt to be the deterrence of others; and here it has been asserted that the justification must fail because victory carries immunity, whether or not the victor was the aggressor, and whatever the measures by which victory was attained.

The argument has a degree of validity but it does not prove enough to prevail. Treason, too, is punishable only when it is abortive; when "it prospers," as the old verse goes, "none dare call it treason"; it is the traitors who call the turn. With respect to war and the manner in which it is conducted, as with respect to treason, there are men who, valuing personal survival, will take account of the contingency of failure. It is to them that the threats are addressed. Moreover, the threat of punishment is not limited in the mode of its operation to the weight that it carries as a factor in decision at the climactic moment of choice. It also operates, and perhaps more significantly, at anterior stages in the patterns of conduct, the dark shadow of organized disapproval eliminating from the ambit of consideration alternatives that might otherwise present themselves in the final competition of choice. These considerations point to some deterrent efficacy; that, and not the assurance of prevention, is all that we can claim for punishment as an instrument of domestic law. It is deemed to be sufficient in municipal affairs, not because of a mathematical calculation of its efficiency, but rather because society, so desperately in need of instrumentalities of prevention, cannot dispense with such potency as condemnation and punishment have.

III

If punishment cannot be dismissed as intrinsically ineffective in the situation with which we are dealing, we must consider whether it was in fact conditioned upon proper grounds.

Putting aside for the moment any special conception of legality, who will assert that the conditions of punishability prescribed by the London Charter are not accurately addressed to the evils incident to war that international society should seek to prevent? The greatest evil is, of course, the initiation of war itself. Once the evil of war has been precipitated, nothing remains but the fragile effort, embodied for the most part in the conventions, to limit the cruelty by which it is conducted. These are the two major branches of the Charter: crimes against peace and violations of the laws and customs of war. Of these two challenges to life and to all that makes life worth living, who will deny that the larger offense is the unjustified initiation of a war?

Goering, having admitted organizing the Nazi program of

slave labor — a plain violation of the conventions and a traditional war crime — defended himself, in effect, by attacking the Hague Conventions as inapplicable to modern war.[2] It would be a mistake to suppose that his point was entirely without substance — though no conception of modern military necessity could have justified what the evidence showed. But is it not clear that the attention that would be accorded to a complaint of this order fails when it is remembered that the military necessity asserted was at best that of his own creation? One who viewed as the basic question for Germany — and I quote Hitler's words — "where the greatest possible conquest could be made at the lowest cost,"[3] had hardly the same position to justify extremes in the use of force as his victims might have, acting in an honest estimate of what was necessary in their own defense. But this is only to demonstrate that the Tribunal was right in declaring that the initiation of a war of aggression "is the supreme international crime."[4]

There are, of course, problems, and difficult ones indeed, in the ultimate definition of aggression — at least under conditions of world organization as they have obtained in the last years. There may be difficult issues in defining the scope of national authority to act in what it conceives to be necessary self-defense — one of the points of our reservation on the Kellogg-Briand Pact. But those issues were not involved in Nuremberg — for not even Hitler, had he stood in the dock, could have asserted against the verified minutes of his own meetings that when he gave the marching orders against Poland he was acting in self-defense. Measured by the Nurem-

[2] 9 *id.* at 362–64.

[3] 22 *id.* at 431, quoting Colonel Hossbach's notes of a conference held 5 November 1937. The notes in German will be found in Document 386–PS, 15 *id.* at 402.

[4] 22 *id.* at 427.

berg evidence the problem of the conditions of punishment did not inhere in the general character of the rules laid down in the London Charter, but rather in the extent of the liability of individuals that those rules undertook to prescribe.

IV

We cannot canvass all the problems of this order, but they can be illustrated by references to the case.

(1) Article 6 (a) of the Charter defined as a crime against peace not only the preparation and initiation of a war of aggression but also the "waging" of such a war. Does this mean that, once it was established that the German war was, in fact, one of aggression, everyone who participated in waging it committed an international crime? If so, every soldier who fought in the Wehrmacht in the field, everyone who participated in war production would, at the least, have been brought within the rule. To be sure, the prosecution disclaimed any such sweeping contention, insisting, especially in the case of the military men, that it was for their part in fomenting and initiating the war and in the perpetration of war crimes that the charges against them had been filed. Common sense would, indeed, rebel at any conception of liability that failed to take adequate account of the actual choice open to particular individuals living within a national state or, to state the same point in a different way, of the compulsions to support a national policy that they may be wholly unable to influence or to change. The point would perhaps be best met if it were recognized that there are cases in which, so far as international sanctions are concerned, justice may require that superior orders be recognized as a complete defense. Whether such orders should constitute a defense or only a mitigation or

neither would, in this view, depend on the actual freedom of choice open to individuals in the society of nations as it exists at the particular time. Since the Charter provision barred such orders as a defense in any case, the Tribunal was forced to deal with the issue in other terms. The conviction of Doenitz of waging a war of aggression, compared with the acquittal of Fritzsche, who functioned as a propagandist during the war, suggests that the Tribunal, extremely sensitive to problems of this kind, actually drew the line in terms of the significance of the role played by the particular individual and the extent of his opportunity for ascertaining the underlying facts about the character of the war.

(2) A similar problem is posed by the affirmation, under the Charter, of liability for conspiracy to wage aggressive war — both as a crime in itself and as a basis of responsibility for substantive offenses committed pursuant to the common plan.

It was, in effect, the submission of the prosecution that the Nazi leaders and their associates were engaged from the start in the furtherance of a program having for its specific objective the attainment of large territorial gains at least in Europe; that from the beginning they were committed to the attainment of those ends by any necessary means — including aggressive wars; that the development of the Nazi Party, the seizure of power, the suppression of free labor, the attack on the Church, the regimentation of youth, the persecution of the Jews and other minorities, the reorganization of the state, rearmament, reoccupation of the Rhineland, Austria, Czechoslovakia and ultimately Poland, and the general war were all contemplated steps in the unfolding of the conspiratorial plan; that after the war began, the plan developed to embrace, as systematic objectives, deportation, pillage, and extermination in general disregard of the laws of war; and, finally, that these objectives were so widely publicized and otherwise generally understood that anyone who occupied an important position in party or government or otherwise rendered significant aid to the Nazi cause would necessarily be guilty of criminal participation.

This position, however valid it might be as to Hitler or Goering or even others, was rejected by the Tribunal in so far as it swept everyone into the net. For conspiracy to be criminal under the Charter, "it must not be too far removed from the time of decision and action"; the Tribunal must find evidence of a specific "concrete plan" and "determine the participants in that concrete plan."[5] Everyone who supports a political program is not to be labeled a criminal conspirator merely because, in the perspective of history, the program seems a coherent unity leading to criminal ends. It is for this reason that eleven of the defendants were acquitted on the charge of conspiracy, leading to the total acquittal of Fritzsche, Von Papen, and Schacht. Shocking it was to give support to Hitler's regime, and repulsive to men of our persuasion, but measured, as it should be, by the standards we would apply to ourselves, more was required to establish complicity in the criminal conspiracy alleged.

It was not enough that Von Papen supported the Nazi accession to power, that he aided the Austrian venture (which, being before Munich, was not charged as an aggressive war), or that he served during the war at Ankara — for it was not shown that he was privy to any of the planning that launched the series of aggressive wars. Schacht was in charge of rearmament until 1937, of the Reichsbank until 1939, and not finally dismissed from the government until 1943 — but a majority of the Tribunal was not satisfied that he was privy

[5] *Id.* at 468.

to the specific purpose of utilizing those armaments for aggressive war. These conclusions involved, of course, the inferences to be drawn from the evidence, and anyone who knows the record will attest the vitality in the judgment of the Tribunal of the principle of reasonable doubt. The point would be indicated less controversially by suggesting a clear case: a welfare officer who concluded that social service was a good even in a Nazi environment, and who did not delude himself as to what Hitler was about, could not have been convicted of criminal participation merely by proving that welfare services contributed to the maintenance of the Nazi hold.

The necessity of such limiting principles is particularly apparent when a charge of criminality pierces the insulation of the national state and the defendants rely heavily on national patriotism to justify their participation in government affairs. It is apparent also for another reason. If liability were asserted in such broad terms that practically everyone within the offending state would sense himself as subject to it, once the die were cast by the initiation of war, the sanctions of the laws of war would have no field of operation. There would, in short, be no incentive for anyone within the country to mitigate the rigors of the conflict or, indeed, to help bring it to an end.

(3) Points such as these apply with special force to the charges leveled against the six organizations. The extraordinary provisions of the Charter on which these charges were based were formulated in the view that it would be practically impossible to enforce responsibility under generally accepted theories of accessorial liability if it were necessary to repeat in every individual case the necessarily elaborate proof of the criminal character of particular organizations and groups. It was concluded, accordingly, that a procedure should be employed to permit the issue of the culpability of organizations

to be determined in a single trial in which their leaders would be individual defendants, reserving to particular members the opportunity, should they be prosecuted for their membership, of adducing any evidence that might free them from personal culpability despite their membership in the criminal group. The justification for the device was that it could work no essential injustice since, on the assumptions made, if the evidence in the major trial had been repeated in any of the individual proceedings, the state of the evidence would be such that the defendant would, in any event, be put to his proof.

However plausible in conception, this aspect of the Nuremberg proceeding proved to be a doubtful element. Two million persons at least were included within the ambit of the charges and, as the organizations were defined by the indictment, there were inescapable ambiguities in the measure of their actual scope. More than this, the underlying theory faced procedural difficulties of major moment as thousands of members of the challenged organizations offered to testify that they were unaware of the criminal purposes alleged and innocent of any criminal acts. Was the Tribunal to try the issues thus presented, and could it undertake to do so without protracting the main proceeding to wholly impossible lengths?

The problem was resolved, in substance, by the criteria employed by the Tribunal to determine criminality.[6] In the first place, it was held to be essential that the organization charged have actual existence as a group entity, so that individuals when they became members understood that they were identifying themselves with a collective purpose. In the second place, it was required that criminal objectives be shown to be the pervasive purpose of the group as a whole and not merely the secret intentions of its leaders or of some isolated portion

6 *Id.* at 500–23.

of the whole. In the third place, in estimating the criminality of group objectives, the Tribunal employed the same limiting conceptions that were addressed to the conspiracy charge as a whole.[7]

The consequence was not only denial of the declaration of criminality as to three of the accused organizations but rigorous limitations of the declarations made with respect to the Gestapo, the S.S., and the Leadership Corps. Some categories of membership were excluded entirely, notably those which terminated prior to 1939. Even more significantly, the membership to be included was redefined in the declaration to comprise only those persons who became or remained members voluntarily with knowledge of the criminal objectives, or who themselves participated in the formulation or execution of criminal plans. In the final result, therefore, the declaration of criminality was all but deprived of significance, for in any subsequent proceeding against individual members it became necessary for the prosecution to establish guilty knowledge or participation; and the proof that would suffice for this purpose would, under ordinary circumstances, suffice to make out an individual case. And this, I submit, was as it should be, for in actual fact, in the then state of knowledge in Germany, there was little excuse for presecuting anyone if the evidence would not establish an individual case. The denazification program applied, of course, to all Germans and was more than sufficient for other situations — but its justification inhered less in punitive considerations than in the simple premise that the Nazis were least eligible to participate in the reconstruction of Germany and most eligible to perform the disagreeable labor involved in cleaning up the debris of the war. Indeed, the Tribunal recommended that anyone convicted only of

[7] See p. 149, *supra*.

membership in an organization declared criminal should, in any event, be treated no more severely than the denazification law allowed.

I have said enough, I trust, to indicate the type of problem involved in the application of the Charter that seems to me to warrant the closest attention as the process of historical inquiry proceeds. Issues of this kind are inherent in any effort to apply international sanctions to individuals; they find their parallel within the nations in the surprisingly universal conceptions of culpability embodied in municipal penal law.

V

It will be said that I have spoken of the Nuremberg trial in terms that ignore the entire controversy and, in a genuine sense, my critic will be right. I have not addressed myself to whether a tribunal of the victors could be impartial, to whether the law of the Charter was *ex post facto*, or whether it was "law" at all. These are, indeed, the issues that have been mooted. But there are elements in the debate that should lead us to be suspicious of the issues as they are drawn in these terms. For most of those who mount the attack on one or another of these contentions hasten to assure us that their plea is not one of immunity for the defendants; they argue only that they should have been disposed of politically, that is, dispatched out of hand. This is a curious position indeed. A punitive enterprise launched on the basis of general rules, administered in an adversary proceeding under a separation of prosecutive and adjudicative powers is, in the name of law and justice, asserted to be less desirable than an *ex parte* execution list or a drumhead court martial constituted in the immediate aftermath of the war. I state my view reservedly when I say that history will accept no conception of law, politics, or justice that supports a submission in these terms. Those who choose to do so may view the Nuremberg proceeding as "political" rather than "legal" — a program calling for the judicial application of principles of liability politically defined. They cannot view it as less civilized an institution than a program of organized violence against prisoners, whether directed from the respective capitals or by military commanders in the field.

I will go further, however, and assert that history would have granted short shrift to a program of summary execution, for such a program is intrinsically unreasonable and could not have been carried out without mistake. Moreover, despite the controversy as to whether the Geneva Convention survives unconditional surrender, when no army remains in the field, I cannot conceive for myself that such a program comports with the Convention's demands. If the execution of prisoners without trial is a war crime while hostilities are in progress, I do not see why it is in any better position when hostilities have come to an end. In my view, Justice Jackson was wrong in arguing that the defendants could point to no other law than the London Charter to assure them any hearing at all.[8] They could point to the Geneva Convention. But the substance of his argument was right. Those who relied upon a treaty for their protection could not argue that treaties were without significance as a basis of liability, if their punishment was otherwise just.

No one who examines the record and the judgment, as most of the commentators have not, will question the disinterestedness of the Tribunal; and those who argue that disinterestedness is inherently impossible in this situation may ask them-

[8] See especially 19 *id.* at 398 and 2 *id.* at 102, 143.

selves why nations that can produce such impartial critics should be intrinsically incapable of producing equally impartial judges. The fact is that the judgment of the Tribunal was mainly a judgment of limitation, its principal operation more significantly that of protecting innocence than that of declaring and punishing guilt. When I speak of "innocence," I mean not only a technical freedom from responsibility under the rules laid down; I mean, more deeply, the exculpation of those who could not justly be declared to be guilty under rules of liability that we would be prepared to apply to ourselves.

No one who is satisfied that the conditions of punishment laid down by the Charter and the Tribunal were essentially just and constructive, in the terms I have previously advanced, will in the end deny them his endorsement on the ground that they were retroactively defined. There is, indeed, too large a disposition among the defenders of Nuremberg to look for stray tags of international pronouncements and reason therefrom that the law of Nuremberg was previously fully laid down. If the Kellogg-Briand Pact or a general conception of international obligation sufficed to authorize England, and would have authorized us, to declare war on Germany in defense of Poland — and in this enterprise to kill countless thousands of German soldiers and civilians — can it be possible that it failed to authorize punitive action against individual Germans judicially determined to be responsible for the Polish attack? To be sure, we would demand a more explicit authorization for punishment in domestic law, for we have adopted for the protection of individuals a prophylactic principle absolutely forbidding retroactivity that we can afford to carry to that extreme. International society, being less stable, can afford less luxury. We admit that in other respects. Why should we deny it here?

VI

There is, however, one point in the debate that we cannot summarily dismiss. It is the point that the punitive enterprise undertaken at Nuremberg applied only to the enemy. My concern on this score is not with the contention that sanctions must for this reason be ineffective, a point that I have previously met. Nor is it with the argument that we have established a precedent that some future victor may invoke against us. If we are guilty of aggression we shall merit its invocation; if we are not, we can ask for no more — not alone for ourselves but for our cause — than the opportunity to establish our innocence that the Nuremberg defendants received. My concern is with the point of equality itself, so important an element of justice — equality in the sense that the sanctions did not apply either to our allies or to ourselves. The Russians could not be put to their defense in relation to Finland or to Poland. We were obliged to present to no Tribunal the considerations we would have advanced to justify the manner in which we exhibited to Japan the power of the atom bomb. This is a genuine difficulty — to which the Tribunal indicated its sensitivity in various ways, such as refusing to assess a penalty against Doenitz for submarine violations that did not differ significantly from our own practice in the Pacific, as attested by Admiral Nimitz. To be sure, the depravity of our enemies and the fact that theirs was the aggression accorded us such large leeway in this connection that our relative moral position was secure. But this is a mitigation rather than a defense to the inequality that Nuremberg involved.

I do not think that the difficulty argues that we should have abstained from the Nuremberg venture and accorded immunity to the guilty defendants, the only terms on which abstinence would have been real. It argues rather that Nuremberg, far more than San Francisco, was the assumption of an irrevocable obligation — to build a world of just law that shall apply to all, with institutions strong enough to carry it into effect. It was, moreover, as Justice Jackson so properly reiterated, an obligation assumed as well by those of our allies who participated in the trial or gave it their sanction by adhering to the Charter. If we succeed in that great venture — and no nation can succeed alone — Nuremberg will stand as a cornerstone in the house of peace. If we fail, we shall hear from the German ruins an attack on the Nuremberg judgment as the second "diktat" of Versailles; and, notwithstanding the goodness of our intentions, we may have no sufficient answer.

INDEX

Index

Index

Index

Index

Bei Fragen zur Produktsicherheit wenden Sie sich bitte an:
If you have any questions regarding product safety,
please contact:

Walter de Gruyter GmbH
Genthiner Straße 13
10785 Berlin
productsafety@degruyterbrill.com